To Ali,

Thank you for y

Keep the fist raised !!!

KAЗ

6/28/14

RAISE YOUR BROWN BLACK FIST

The Political Shouts of an Angry Afro Latino

Kevin Alberto Sabio

authorHOUSE®

AuthorHouse™
1663 Liberty Drive
Bloomington, IN 47403
www.authorhouse.com
Phone: 1-800-839-8640

First published by AuthorHouse   2/19/2010

ISBN: 978-1-4490-6989-6 (e)
ISBN: 978-1-4490-6987-2 (sc)
ISBN: 978-1-4490-6988-9 (hc)

Library of Congress Control Number: 2010902353

Printed in the United States of America
Bloomington, Indiana

This book is printed on acid-free paper.

An Introduction

My beginnings started humbly enough; the youngest of three children of Honduran Garifuna immigrant parents. We were born and raised here in the United States, planting our familial roots in New York City, specifically in the Borough of Brooklyn. We started out in the housing projects of East New York, moving into our childhood home in East Flatbush at the respective ages of 9, 7, and 6. The seeds of my political growth were being planted, even way back then. My parents were not radicals by any means; but we were never taught to believe that our nationality was our race. We were always made aware of our Black/African heritage, and always celebrated our Blackness. We were never raised to be ashamed to call ourselves Black. I remember many times when we celebrated Black History Month, watched the documentary "Eyes on the Prize" when it came on PBS, and being affected by the many events concerning Black people during our upbringing. We always fit in with other Black people, despite the fact that my family spoke Spanish.

I didn't reach my political maturity until the age of 16 in the early 1990s. It was during that era when many great things were happening. On college campuses throughout the country, Black students were calling for the inclusion of Black/Africana Studies into the curriculum, not just as electives. You also had the rise of

Afrocentric thought permeating in the community. And the biggest influence for me....was the rise of 'conscious' rap music. The artists of the time spoke of nationalist concepts that were foreign to me, but alluring at the same time. They spoke of leaders and groups that rarely get spoken of, if ever at all. They spoke of celebrating and expressing your culture, and claiming (or reclaiming) your African heritage. What really set me on my political path was reading "The Autobiography of Malcolm X" by Alex Haley, and "Souls on Ice" by Eldridge Cleaver. From that point on, I never looked back.

Most of my political activity took place during my college years. At the colleges that I attended over the years, I was involved with a number of student organizations during my times there. For two out of the three colleges that I attended, I was on some sort of probationary status because of my political activity (moreso my bad temper). There are many times when I mix my political beliefs with my art, infusing them into my screenplays and other projects that I'm involved with, also having involved myself in the Black Film Festival circuit for 5 years. There are also many political battles that I've fought over the years for the betterment of my people. I am unapologetic in what I believe in, and that has garnered me just as much respect as it has resentment among my peers. I try to incorporate everything that I've learned into my everyday lifestyle, and try to teach others that there is an alternative.

Perhaps I am more of a soldier in the cause than I care to admit, though I know that we all can't be fighters. We are all soldiers in different ways. While some of us can physically fight, others can teach, while others still can be thinkers or healers. Others are also good at using the written word to get their point(s) across to supports, nonbelievers, and the uninitiated alike. That is pretty much where I fit into all of this. I had never expected to get into journalism; I found it to be boring and unentertaining. I never realized just how powerful my words could be in that arena, or how much of an impact that they would have. I've always wanted to be able to reach the masses on some higher level with my words, though I had wanted to do it in a totally different arena; wanting more to 'edu-tain' the masses.

These collections of my writings gathered in this volume were written when I was associated with a website called Blacktino.net; an E-zine that I am no longer affiliated with. I was approached by the creator(s) of the site back in March of 2007, in which they were looking for writers to post original content for their e-magazine. I initially balked at the idea, not having any prior journalistic experience (save one semester for class credit), nor having the inclination to do journalism-type work. After a bit of persuading from the site creator(s), I finally decided to take them up on their offer. The position of Contributing Writer that I held was unpaid; I did it more for the recognition. Our relationship was one of mutual benefit during my time with their site. We officially parted ways in August of 2008, not on the best of terms. There were a lot of behind-the-scenes issues that caused our unhappy disassociation, issues that I will not go into in this volume. What I *will* say about our parting is…that my conscience is clear about this situation, and why it ended. Can the other party say the same?

In this book is a collection of two article series that I wrote while working as a Contributing Writer for the site. The first series, titled Black vs. Brown, is an eight-part series that deals with the supposed friction between the Black and Latino communities, and putting this supposed conflict in a historical perspective. The second series, titled Black Thoughts, is (currently) a seven-part series that focuses on why Latinos of African descent should embrace the ideology of Black Nationalism/Pan Africanism. Only the first three articles of this particular series were posted on Blacktino.net; the subsequent articles in this series were posted elsewhere, on websites such as **Afropresencia.com**, and **Assatashakur.org**. Both of these series have been well received, and have been re-published/re-posted on numerous sites, and parts of <u>Black Thoughts</u> have even been translated into French and Spanish. For their inclusions in this book, the articles have been reedited for informational and grammatical errors made during their original posting/publishing.

I would like to extend thanks to the many friends and family members (all of the Sabios, Avilas, Castros, Garcias, Melendezes, and the rest) who have always been very supportive of my writing efforts. I would also like to extend feelings of undying gratitude to the many ancestors, comrades, and sisteren that I have met in my political journeys (Robert Oriyama'at, Kamean Daniels, Karen Juanita Carrillo, Jan Calloway, Janet "Queen Nzinga" Taylor, Tracey "Amachi" Robinson, Koblah Atiba, "Book Man" Mike, to name a few) learning as much as I could from them. I would also like to thank the many fans that I have made along the way (Tony, Chase, Veronica, Carmen, James "Moorbey" Harris, Lynx Garcia, Bruno Gaston), for without your support, none of this would ever be possible.

Lastly, I must give respect to the people at Blacktino.net. Had I not agreed to write for their site, these writings might not even exist at all. Though my feelings haven't changed much positively towards them, I must give respect where respect is due.

Part I

Black vs. Brown: Where's the beef?

By: *Kevin Alberto Sabio*

In this hostile environment against immigrants, one voice that seems to be generally ignored by the mainstream press is the impact that this illegal immigration has had on the Black community. In reading the Black press, those in the Black community feel doubly affected by this influx of immigrants; neighborhoods that were once historically Black are now becoming 'Latinized'. There are also claims being made that illegal immigrants are stealing away jobs from Blacks. My question to all of this hoopla is...are they *really* giving us *that* much trouble?

One of the first points that I would like to make is that if the government REALLY wanted to get a handle on the immigration issue, they would have done it by now. If they can succeed in destroying any type of independent nationalist movements by the various communities of color, then they can stop a few migrants from entering the country, or exceeding their stay.

Secondly, the illegal immigrants aren't destroying our neighborhoods; the government has been doing a fine job of that over the past forty or fifty years. Illegal immigrants didn't cause 'White Flight' and the redlining of banks to would-be business owners/ home owners of color. Immigrants don't cause gentrification in urban neighborhoods. If anything, having an immigrant group coming into a depressed neighborhood might actually help to revitalize the community and cause it to thrive.

Let's get to the issue of jobs. When you talk about immigrants stealing jobs from Blacks, who are you talking about? I'm a Latino of African descent, born and raised in the United States. You have Black immigrants from the Caribbean, and from the motherland. Should they be thrown into the mix when you talk about these thieving immigrants that take jobs away from African Americans? The problem doesn't lie with the illegals that are here; the issue lies with the employers who would rather hire them because they know that they can get away with exploiting them. Most immigrants are just happy to have a job so that they can support themselves, and their family. They're not as willing to speak out against injustices that would go on at the workplace. American-born workers understand their rights, and wouldn't hesitate to report their employer to a union, or even a government agency for any transgressions. If you were a grimy business person, who would YOU hire to work for you? I think that the answer is obvious.

I'm not blind or naïve. I have had a number of occasions in my life where I have met some really arrogant immigrants who act like they are better than native born African Americans. They have no idea of the history and legacy that we have in this country, and continue to treat us with utter disrespect. Of course, karma has a way of coming back around, and slapping you with a really hard dose of reality. Some would say that Arabs in the Muslim community are now feeling those affects since the 9-11 attacks.

Blacks and Latinos actually share a long political history in this country. Many Latino political movements in the 1960's and '70's were inspired by organizations started by African Americans, such as the impact that the Black Panther Party for Self Defense had on the Brown Berets and Young Lords Party. There wasn't always this divisiveness between the two communities. Integration has helped to fracture the Black community itself; imagine its effect on Black/ Brown relations?

I suggest that we all do a bit of homework before we start to fly off on the deep end. Before we start to spout rhetoric that isn't even of our own thinking, we need to take a minute and analyze who is going to benefit from all of this infighting. Blacks and Latinos can shout and holler at each other until we're blue in the face, the question still begs: who's benefiting from this? Black people don't control the economy in our own neighborhoods. Latinos may be able to pool their own resources to make certain advances, but without citizenship, they can only go so far. Not to mention, you don't have a national Latino political agenda that unites the entire Latino community regardless of your nationality. Who wins? The Powers-That-Be that have been in control all along. We tear at each other, weakening our own forces, while they remain strong and in control. Spike Lee said it best in his classic film School Daze......WAKE UP!!!!!!!!!!!!

BLACK VS. BROWN 2: THE NEXT LEVEL

By: *Kevin Alberto Sabio*

I had previously written about this issue before, with plans on making this a series of articles. I ended up getting sidetracked a bit, covering other issues in my writing. With the climate the way that it is between the two communities, I felt that it was imperative to readdress this issue.

I feel that my perspective is a unique one on many different levels. On the one hand, it was the location where I grew up and who I got to grow up with. As I've stated before, I feel very fortunate to have been born and raised in New York City. Being a 'melting pot', I got the opportunity to be around people of many different nationalities and spiritual persuasions. I grew up with other Latinos on my block, and was classmates with them all throughout my academic career. My friends were from Puerto Rico, the Dominican Republic, Colombia, Panama, and many other places throughout the Caribbean and Latin America.

On the other hand, you have my unique heritage. Culturally, I am a Latino; my heritage is from Honduras. Ethnically, I am African. That alone confuses the hell out of many people. I'm not fluent in

Spanish; actually I speak very little. I don't speak with an accent, or 'act' Latino (whatever the hell *that* means!). When people find out about my background, they always get these confused looks on their faces, Latinos and Blacks alike. I almost always get the same response from people: "But...but....you're BLACK??!!" Of course, me being me, I always give the same smartass response; "Yeah, you see...during the time of slavery, they sent the Africans *all over* the hemisphere... not just to what became the United States."

Labels

I've been into race consciousness and political activity since my teen years; since I was sixteen to be exact (I'm now 33). I've always identified strongly with my African roots, taking up many Black causes. I'm just as likely to be racially profiled by the cops (which has happened *many* times already), and be referred to by the N-word as the next brother or sister. In my early days of activism, I would prefer to use the term 'Afro-Hispanic', paying full homage to my background. It wasn't until the 90s when the term 'Latino' soon began to be coined as a form of self determination. The more I thought about it, the more it made sense. My family comes from *Latin America*, therefore, I'm a Latino. There is no country in existence called Hispana, so why should I be referred to as a Hispanic? Not to mention, Hispanic was an identifying term that was *imposed* on us. So while African Americans were reaffirming and reclaiming their African roots and identity, Latinos were doing the same thing. We should be free to determine who we are, and how we identify ourselves.

Black/Brown Relations

This made me even more politically active, now also taking up Latino causes, and working on establishing and/or solidifying Black/Brown coalitions. Not only would I research Black political organizations, but made an effort to learn about other Latino cultures, and Latino excursions into political activity. It was through there that I learned about groups like the Young Lords Party, and the Brown Berets. Growing up in NYC, the Black and Puerto Rican communities have always had a long history of working together and fighting for political causes. This was just a continuation of what I had always seen and learned.

My political activity continued on throughout my college years, and currently in my personal life. I have to admit, I've seen my share of fractures in these Black/Brown coalitions. As I've stated before; integration has seriously fractured the Black community, what do you think its effects are on Black/Brown political relations? As of late, you've been hearing a lot about friction between the two communities, especially concerning immigration, and its impact on the Black community. To reiterate, I've had my fair share of negative experiences with racist Latinos who have absolutely NO respect for African Americans. I've been given the cold shoulder, and been treated with nasty attitudes by my 'fellow' Latinos before. You'd be surprised at the shocked looks that would hit their faces when they find out that I'm not African American per se. As it is, I have a deep hatred for my former employer; a white Cuban. He was a two-faced racist to the core. He treated his Black employees like dirt, myself included. The only difference between them and I, is that I would fight him back after he pulled some crap. I have no qualms about calling him what he is; a dirty spic. What's that old Latino saying? "And what does your grandmother look like?"

I also have to admit, that on the other side, I've heard some things fly out of the mouths of African Americans that can be considered deeply racist.

Send them back where they came from!
They're stealing our jobs!
They're benefiting off of programs that we started!

These people breed like cockroaches!
They come over here, and don't want to learn the language!

I'm not going to say that African Americans don't have a legitimate beef; to a certain extent, they do. But, I also won't stand for wonton ignorance to be spread around, and go unchallenged.

You say send them back to where they came from? They're being exploited in their own country by American corporations. Their governments are corrupted by these same corporations, and have historically been overthrown whenever they challenged American corporate and colonial interests. Obviously if it was all gravy in their own country, they wouldn't be risking life and limb to come here.

They're stealing our jobs? No, they're not. They were never *our* jobs to begin with. These jobs were the ones that the Powers-That-Be *allowed* us to have. If we were smart, we would take a cue from the Jim Crow days, and create our own economy. Garvey said it, Stokely Carmichael said it; hell, he wrote a whole book on it called "*Black Power*". His work was even followed up by Dr. Amos Wilson in his book "*Blueprint for Black Power*". Did we listen? No. We too busy fighting over the little crumbs that they throw at us right now.

Are they benefiting from programs that African Americans had created? Yes. Whose fault is that? Well…the Powers-That-Be, for one. Also, blame the African American community for sleeping. We hardly ever pressure the government to make good on any of the 'concessions' that we won during the Civil Rights Movement. If we were truly citizens of this country A) we wouldn't have to fight for Civil Rights, our natural citizenship gives us those rights. And B) we wouldn't need special programs to force the government to provide us equal opportunities in the fields of business, education, home ownership, etc.

The rest of the stuff is just about stupidity and arrogance. I won't even dignify it with a rebuttal.

The Story continues...

Since my relocation to the south, a lot of people have been able to benefit from my experiences concerning Latinos. Many people down here have only experienced Black and White their whole lives; throwing Latinos into the paradigm is new to them. Especially when they learn about my background, I'm able to help break down the real issues of the situations, and give them a bit more insight about Latinos, and our history. There is still a level of uneasiness that exists, understandably so. Racism in the south was much more blatant that it was in the north. There is a conditioning that exists down here in the minds of the Black community; after generations of subjugation by Whites, they see the rising Latino population as a threat. We have to be able to get beyond that, and deal with the *real* issue at hand; the complete control over the resources that the Powers-That-Be have. The story continues.....

BLACK VS. BROWN 3: The Color Line

By: *Kevin Alberto Sabio*

I remember a discussion that I had gotten into during my college days. I was hanging out with a fellow Latino of a lighter hue, when this person admitted to me that they didn't like Black people. After I got over my initial shock over the statement, I remember giving this person a funny look. The person paused, and must have read the look on my face, and basically said, "But not you...you're alright. You're not one of them."

HUH?!

One issue that doesn't get talked about very often when dealing with the Latino community, is the issue of racism *within* the Latino community. Let us not forget, slavery existed in Latin America just as it did in what later became the United States. A Plantation society existed there, just as it did in North America. Slavery in Latin America may not have been as extreme as it was in the Unites States, but quite obviously the effects of that past are bound to still be evident in the culture in this day and age. There is this myth that exists that Latinos are one big racially mixed family. To a certain extent we are. BUT...that doesn't mean that we don't have issues dealing with race and racism. Look at what the effects of slavery and the plantation system have on American society; you think that it wouldn't affect Latinos?

I've had dealing with other Afro-Latinos who would fight you to the death if you dare to call them Black. They would claim their nationality as their race, rather than call themselves Black or African. I've also had dealings with Latinos who were damn near White, proudly proclaiming their African heritage. In certain parts of the Latino community, you have the issue of skin color; a family member with dark skin is often ridiculed, or treated somewhat as an outcast. Tienes pelo malo... 'You have bad hair' if your hair is naturally kinky. In Latino society, if your African roots are very pronounced, it's a bad thing that needs to be denounced. Gee...why does that sound familiar...?

Much of Latino society doesn't embrace its African heritage. They are more than willing to promote and embrace the indigenous parts of their heritage, celebrating the peoples that occupied the lands before the coming of the Europeans. Very few embrace or acknowledge their ties to the continent of Africa. That is quite foolish, since the immense influence that African culture has on Latino culture is quite obvious. Our Indigenous and European heritage will get the bulk of the representation when talking about Latino culture, yet our African heritage gets treated like an unwanted, bastard child.

You have those descriptions that Latino people use when referring to someone of a darker skin-tone, or Black people in general: Moreno/a, Trigueno, Niche, or even the offensive Mayate (which basically means the N-word in Spanish). I would bristle when my lighter complexioned Latino friends would frivolously throw the word 'Moreno' around when talking about Black people. They would jovially say, "Oh...it's not offensive", and continue to use the word. Basically, you're calling me 'darkie'. I don't appreciate that. I know a whole lot of Black people and Afro Latinos who don't appreciate it, either.

I'm also sick and tired of not being recognized as a Latino because I'm Black. Latinos don't all look white, or Indian; we come in an assortment of shapes, sizes and COLORS. I know a WHOLE lot of other Afro Latinos who will cosign with me on this issue. I'm proud of my African roots, and embrace my African heritage, but don't deny me being a part of the culture just based on what I physically look like. I probably know more about your own heritage that you do, just because I read and study. I may not have a great command over the Spanish language, but I make it a point to learn about the history and culture of my people.

Remember the 'Latin Explosion' in the late Nineties? Notice how all of the big music stars that got promoted looked very European? J-Lo and Shakira dyed their hair blonde. Ricky Martin and Marc Anthony were the poster boys for that movement; the whitest looking Latinos that they could find. Even with Rock en Espanol, they all had that European appeal to them. They even tried to include non-Latinos into that phenomenon like Penelope Cruz. She's a European from Spain! Not ONE dark skinned Latino got promoted during that whole fiasco. Yeah sure, we got lucky with a few Afro Latina beauty pageant winners getting thrown in, but even that got very little exposure. If anything, it caused more controversy than progress. Even with the crop of Latino film festivals now popping up, you don't see African descended Latinos being represented in the films. You'd have to go to a Black film festival to see us represented, whether in the storyline, or a documentary about us. Apparently, we have a long way to go.

Before we start hating on others, how about learning to love ourselves first? We need to embrace ALL parts of our heritage. If you have a hatred for Black people, you have hatred for yourself. I would suggest that people learn the true history of Latin America, and rethink these animosities that they have. We need to deprogram ourselves from these lies and myths about us, and truly embrace all of who we are. I think Dr. Joy Leary summed it up best in her book *Post Traumatic Slave Syndrome....* "how can you expect a people to 'get over it' (slavery), when all you did was take off the chains, and never provided any type of therapy for them to deal with the trauma that they experienced?"

BLACK VS. BROWN 4: Knowledge Of Self

By: *Kevin Alberto Sabio*

Imagine my surprise when I discovered how widely circulated my articles were. I hadn't realized how far reaching my words really were, and how many people were actually touched by what I had said, whether positively or negatively. I can only extend my thanks to my editors for reaching out to me, and providing me with the opportunity to have my voice heard. I never initially intended to get involved in journalism (despite a former college professor's prodding during my college days), and to see the impact that my words are having on the masses is very rewarding.

This leads me to my latest musings in this series. As I had accidentally discovered how far reaching my articles were (not just this series), I came across a number of negative comments regarding this particular series, posted both on the home site for my articles (much love Blacktino.net!!!), and on a particular 'Latino' website. The negative comment posted on the BNN site was written by an African American who basically went on a racist rant about Mexicans. On this particular 'Latino' website, I was basically accuse of being a self-hating, angry Black Nationalist who was trying to impose his own racist views on race on the majority of the "proud" Latino community, and of denying my own Latino heritage. In both cases, the posters proved the very point that I've been trying to make with these articles. Ignorance is abundant on both sides…not to mention a lack of reading comprehension on the part of the commentators.

There was a self-proclaimed 'proud Boricua' on this particular 'Latino' website that made some rather dubious comments about "Blacks trying to jump on the Latino bandwagon" when they need help in numbers, and stating that the majority of Latinos don't have any Black/African blood in them. On the latter part of his comment, he's only partially correct. Notice that I said partially. As for the part about Blacks trying to jump on the Latino bandwagon when they need help in numbers….please cut the CRAP! If you knew anything about your history, you would know that Blacks and Puerto Ricans have worked together politically for a number of decades. Puerto Ricans were no more spared from racism and bigotry than African Americans in this country. As a 'proud Boricua', you should know that. Or, are you one of those Americanized Puerto Ricans who doesn't know anything about their own history, whether on the Puerto Rican mainland, or in the United States?

Let me get back to the issue at hand. The main reason behind the beef between the African American and Latino communities is A) ignorance of each other's history and culture, and B) being pitted against each other by this White Supremacist system that has control over all of the resources in this country, and has us fighting over scraps. I'm not trying to 'blame all of our problems on Whitey' as I was accused of doing on this particular 'Latino' website. Black and Latino neighborhoods across this country are being gentrified at an alarming rate, and guess who's moving in? Not us! Banks have been involved in redlining scandals for decades, denying Black and Latino homeowners and business people. Who runs those banks? They've been attacking Affirmative Action regarding enrollment of people of color into the universities of this country. Who do you think that affects, hmm? I rest my case on that point. If you are too Deaf, Dumb, and Blind to understand that, then you've truly bought into this wicked system, and nothing that I say or write will change your mind.

There is enough blame to go around as far as the reasons for the schisms between the two communities. You have Latinos with ingrained racist beliefs about African Americans who emigrate here, and treat them in a disrespectful manner. They end up benefiting from programs that African Americans fought for and had instituted during the Civil Rights Era, and then look their noses down on that community. At the same time, we in the Black community can be very disrespectful to other ethnic groups as well. We chide them for not being able to speak English. We make fun of them for being different from us. We can be disruptive and disrespectful to them in their place of business. I can go on and on, but I choose not to. The fact is that neither side is innocent in this supposed conflict. The Black poster on BNN made a comment about Mexicans immigrating to the States, forming gangs, and killing innocent Black children. Was his voice as loud when it was Black gangs intimidating and killing innocent Mexicans, and other Latinos? I think not.

A coalition between the two communities is necessary on many fronts. We live in an institutionalized racist system, whether you acknowledge it or not. We also have more in common than we realize, both politically and culturally. Working on a united front is nothing new to our communities. I applaud the efforts of someone like Rosa Clemente who is a member of the Malcolm X Grassroots Movement. Since moving out of New York, I miss hearing her co-hosting her radio show. I try to hit up her website as often as I can. As I had stated previously, groups like the Young Lords Party and Brown Berets were greatly influenced by the Black Panther Party for Self Defense. Cesar Chavez was heavily influenced by Dr. Martin

Luther King, and his stance on nonviolence. Also, the National Council for La Raza is known in certain circles as the Latino version of the NAACP. Also, the Black community is just as concerned about immigration as Latinos. We're not all from the United States, you know. We're not as far apart on some issues as it seems.

As for culture, I can point you to the works of such notable scholars as Dr. Arlene Torres, Prof. Victor Vega, and Dr. Marta Moreno-Vega. Dr. Torres' book *"Blackness in Latin American and the Caribbean"* takes an in-depth look at the African lineage in Latin American society. I would also like to point out Chris Rodriguez' *"Latino Manifesto"*, also an excellent read. Roberto Santiago's *"Boricuas"* gives an in-depth look into Puerto Rican history and culture. Patrick Carroll has his book *"Blacks in Colonial Vera Cruz"*, about the Black presence in Mexico. I could go on and on. The information is out there, you just have to seek it. Just like you have issues of race in the Latino community, so too in the Black community. Anybody remember the 'paper bag' test? We're not as color struck as we were a good twenty years ago, but it still exists, especially in the popular media. You don't believe me? Watch a music video sometime...

This issue isn't about one-upmanship, or one side losing out for the other side to gain something. Both communities are facing bitter resistance from the Powers-That-Be. Since our numbers can't necessarily be contained, we're pitted against each other to distract us from reaching our true goals. This country has NEVER been fair to either community, and history has proven that. If you are too assimilated and integrated into this system to believe that, then I'm not speaking to you. I'm speaking to those who recognize the real issues that confront us, and are willing to work to make this country, and this world, a better place. Having a better sense of knowledge of self can help to do that. It really helps to know what you're talking about when dealing with these types of issues.

BLACK VS. BROWN 5: History's Mystery

By: *Kevin Alberto Sabio*

There are two incidents that I remember from my past that have really stuck with me until this day. The first incident was a day in my late teens/early twenties when I was out with some people I knew back in Brooklyn. I was out with a former comrade, his girlfriend, and her cousin. The cousin and I were vibing together, being ideologically like-minded. There was a pause in the conversation, and my former comrade and I noticed a small group of very attractive Latinas walking by across the street. Being the healthy males that we are, we watched them as they passed us by. The cousin got highly offended by this, and said, "Don't you be looking at them Puerto Ricans! You need to be sticking with the sisters!" That kinda threw me, considering the fact that those girls were just as dark, if not darker, than *she* was in complexion.

The other incident was a few years ago, during the time of the so-called 'Latin Explosion'. There was a report in the news about Latinos having passed, or about to surpass, African Americans as the new 'majority' minority in the U.S. Numerous articles were written about it in the mainstream and Black press alike. There were those that panicked, and called this a travesty, whooping and hollering about how detrimental an effect this would be for the African American community. Those who traveled in the same political circles that I did gave a uniform shrug and said, "So what? What has that status ever gotten *us*?"

I want to be able to deal with this issue from a fresh perspective. I don't want to repeat what others before me have said, nor continue to repeat myself from what I had written previously in other articles. What can *I* say that hasn't been mentioned before? What new information can *I* bring to this discussion? What new perspectives can *I* bring to help to enlighten others towards this issue plaguing both communities, and bring an end to the friction? When in doubt, look towards the past.

There has been a lot of friction between the African American and Latino communities in the Southwest. African Americans complain that Latinos (specifically Mexicans) are coming into their neighborhoods, and taking over. My question to that is...were we ever *that* populous in the Southwest? According to history, the American Southwest used to be at least half (if not 2/3) of the country of Mexico. After the Mexican-American War in the 1840s, all of the territories from Texas to California were ceded to the United States, with not many of them becoming slave-holding states. Not to mention the fact that African Americans were still in bondage until after 1865; the close of the American Civil War (slavery in Mexico had been abolished in the late 1820s). We started migrating to other parts of the country afterwards, especially to escape racism in the Deep South (the Klan, Red Shirt Army, Night Riders, race riots, etc).

Let's get back to Incident #2 that I spoke of in the beginning of this article. When they stated that Latinos are/will be the new 'majority' minority, does that include someone that looks like me? Are Afro Latinos included into that mix? When you talk of African Americans, are you excluding other African descended people that were born here, like Afro Caribbean people and Continental Africans?

22

What exactly makes one African American? At what point do other African descended people *become* African Americans? Sounds a bit like propagandist bullshit to me. What makes this sad is that you actually had a number of people in the African American community falling for this crap.

Let's not forget, once the country was legally desegregated, we started abandoning the Black community to live next to the White folks. We suffered an economic and intellectual drain in our community when the elite of the Black community left to move to the suburbs, and other formerly all-White neighborhoods. Not to mention the trickery of the local politicians and economic community, the Black community suffered greatly: redlining from banks, political redistricting, eminent domain, Highway projects, service cuts, and so on. That has helped to destroy the Black community worse than *any* incoming immigrant group.

This isn't about bashing any one group. This also isn't about one group trying/needing to kiss another's ass. Both sides have made a lot of stupid, inconsiderate, and insensitive statements regarding the other on this issue. I've heard a lot of racial talk fly out of the mouths of African Americans that have really angered me considering my heritage. At the same time, I've been dealing with racism from other Latinos for most of my life. I've stated this before; you put me in with a group of brothers from around the way, you'll never be able to pick me out.

I've had a few brothers from the West Coast challenge my stance on this issue, claiming that I can't compare the racism suffered in California perpetrated by the Latino community there to the one(s) that exist in New York. I seriously beg to differ. If anything, I think that it's *MUCH WORSE* in New York than in California. Your beef is mainly with Latinos from Mexico, or of Mexican descent. In New York, we have the *ENTIRETY* of Latin America to deal with. We have Puerto Ricans, Dominicans, Colombians, Venezuelans, Cubans,

Ecuadorians, and more recently, Mexicans. The excuse given was that the Latino population that exists in New York is mostly black, and therefore doesn't apply. You obviously didn't read the third part to my series called The Color Line. I dare you to call one of them Black to their face; see what happens. It doesn't matter what the person's nationality is if they already have prejudice and hatred in their heart. Plus, you have self hatred that exists in the Black community; you think that that couldn't apply to the Latino community as well?

Our histories are long and intertwined. We've fought in the Mexican war for independence (as both slaves and Freedmen). We've fought in the Mexican-American War (as Freedmen) for the Mexicans. We've fought in the Spanish-American War (as the Buffalo Soldiers), freeing Florida, Puerto Rico, and Cuba from the grips of Spain. The Maroons kept the Colonial Powers at bay in their quest for freedom (shout out to all of my Garifuna people). We're not as far apart as we think. I think that if we take the time to *really* understand what the main issues are in this conflict, we can come to an easy resolution. We're not blood enemies; we never were. We've worked together before towards each other's benefit; we can do it again.

BLACK VS. BROWN 6:
Competition is None

By: *Kevin Alberto Sabio*

One of the main sticking points in this supposed conflict between our two communities is the scarcity of jobs, and the fact that African Americans feel that the incoming Latino immigrants (whether legal or illegal) are taking those jobs away that rightfully belong to them. There is also the feeling that Latinos are encroaching onto other societal territories that used to be predominated by African Americans and are in a sense are pushing them out, or making them obsolete. These points, among others, should be thoroughly examined, and put into their proper prospective.

Jobs/Employment

So, exactly which jobs exist that only African Americans can do? I'm always at a loss whenever I hear this particular statement. Personally, it makes it sound as if we are supposed to be genetically predisposed to do a particular task that no other race of people can do. And which jobs are they taking away from us, exactly? I know plenty of brothers and sisters who work at city jobs; bus drivers, sanitation workers, DMV, social services, etc. Are they swiping those jobs from us? And, since when are low paying, low-skilled blue collar labor jobs relegated *only* to African Americans? Last time I checked, it wasn't up to *us* as far as who got hired at certain low-skill level jobs. If a grimy business owner chooses to hire an immigrant (Latino or otherwise) over a citizen just so that he can financially exploit that worker at these jobs, then that's on the business owner. You need to hold that business owner accountable, not blame the immigrant worker.

Another thing is that we don't pool our resources together like we should, and create our own economy. If we created our own economy, we can create jobs for our own people. We wouldn't have to rely on the mainstream society to provide us with jobs. If this sounds like I'm talking about nationalism, it's because I AM! Other immigrant groups that come to this country practice some form of nationalism. That's how you are able to have certain communities (and I do mean communities, not just neighborhoods) that are able to prosper in some of this country's larger inner cities. You have a number of Chinatowns, Little Italys, Little Koreas, and so on, that exist in some of America's major cities. Immigrants will come here, pool their resources together, and the next thing you know, their community has grown significantly.

For African Americans, we haven't practiced that type of solidarity since Jim Crow. We're so happy to integrate with massa, or be the HNIC, that we choose not to work together, or support each other economically. People would constantly look at me funny if I were to tell them to support a Black-owned business, or just 'buy Black'. They would consider my way of thinking irrelevant, and outdated. Yet, they are the first ones to complain that you have all of these 'foreign' businesses in our neighborhoods, and that we couldn't get any Black-owned businesses in our own neighborhoods to save our lives. Well, did you support them when they *were* in the neighborhood? Do you at least *try* to make it a habit to support a Black business? I rest my case...

Sports

I've been reading recently in certain Black publications about the lack of African American ballplayers in Major League Baseball, and how that has now become a major concern. They site the influx of Latino and Asian ballplayers now in the game, and how the lack of African American representation is cause for alarm. It was a bit curious on my part, because they kept saying African American, and not Black. Oh wait, that's right...you *do* have Black ballplayers in Major League Baseball! They're just not 'American'. Well...North American, I should say...

Remember Orlando "El Duque" Hernandez? He used to pitch for the New York Yankees. He was a pitching phenom out of Cuba. Both he and his brother Livan Hernandez defected from Cuba to play professionally in the United States. They were Afro Cubans. How about Sammy Sosa, one of three people to break Roger Maris' single-season homerun record? Can you deny his African roots? There are many others that I can site that are playing, or have played in the League. At the same time, is there really an interest among African Americans to *want* to play professional baseball? The number of African Americans that I have questioned about this issue have all stated how boring they found baseball to be. They would barely watch the World Series, much less the regular season. They would always be more interested in college or pro basketball, or be more caught up on the current football season. And now, with the influx of immigrants from the Caribbean, Latin America, and continental Africa, soccer is gaining a growing fan base in the U.S.

Also, Little League teams are usually funded by the local city; if they cut the budget, they can't play a season. Not to mention, it takes a lot of space, people, and equipment to play a game. Playing one-on-

one can get you pitching and hitting…what about the fielding aspect of the game? With basketball, all that you need is a ball and a hoop; with football, all you really need is the ball itself. There were many days in my youth that I remember playing crateball, or street football. Baseball was a wee bit more complicated to organize…

Competition is none…

So, who are we really fighting against? Should you be less upset if the immigrant you were passed over for was Black, or European? Let's not try to act as if Latinos are the only ones that are coming into this country, whether legally or not. You have Europeans sneaking into this country just as much as everyone else. This is nothing more than about both exploitation, and control. We're not losing our homes, jobs, or neighborhoods to anyone (well…except to the Powers-That-Be, of course). If we were truly handling our business, none of this would even be an issue. We showed how much of an economic force we could be during the times of segregation. Because of the fact that we've become so individualistic now, we've become defenseless to those that choose to exploit and suppress us. Maybe if we practiced a little more solidarity, we wouldn't be dealing with some of these issues that concern us today. These issues are not new to us, and are not that complicated to figure out. These are the same old tactics, just dressed up in a new outfit. Let's trying learning from our mistakes for once, shall we?

BLACK VS. BROWN 7:
What's A Brother to Do?

By: *Kevin Alberto Sabio*

What's a brother to do?
What's a bro' to do…what's a bro' to do…what's a bro' to do?
What's a bro' to do…what's a bro' to do…what's a bro' to do?
What's a brother to do?
* • The Future Sound (NYC rap group), circa 1992

People kill me! Ain't technology grand?

Now, why choose to open this particular article with those particular statements? Simply because it amazes me that as smart as people can be to be able to use this particular technology (the internet), they can make the most asinine of statements about any particular issue. As I had stated before in the article subtitled "Knowledge of Self" in the series, I had discovered that my stories have been reposted on various other websites besides Blacktino.net, Latino and otherwise. I have received both praise and criticism for what I've written. Not to say that I can't take criticism, but some of these people end up proving the very points that I've been making since first writing the series. There's a lot of ignorance floating around on both sides, and a lot of people talking a lot of junk online. Personally, I just think that they're suffering from ITGS (Internet Tough Guy/Girl Syndrome). It's easy to anonymously log onto a website and talk trash about a particular topic; would you have the same gumption to say whatever it is that you stated to a living person standing right in front of you? I doubt it...

On one particular website, a woman named "Jenny" commented on my article subtitled "Competition is None" on another website, and had accused me of spreading 'Hispanic propaganda' in the article. Okay...quite obviously you suffer from a lack of reading comprehension. Had you read the article correctly, you would have known that, if I was spreading *any* type of propaganda, it was **BLACK NATIONALIST** propaganda! You know...the part where I said, and I quote, "If it sounds like I'm talking about nationalism...it's because I AM!"? You must not have seen that part; you were too busy going on some B.S. rant condoning your prejudice against Latinos as if they are the bane of African American existence in this country. They're not stealing our jobs, sister-girl...the Powers That Be have been doing a bang up job of taking jobs away from us for generations. Where's your big mouth on that? Oh, and by the way....don't call me Hispanic. Would you like it if I called you Colored or Negro?

On another website, another poster had commented on Dr. Nicholas Vaca, and his book "Presumed Alliance". Apparently, Dr. Vaca has a different take on the schism between the two communities. I have heard of Dr. Vaca and his book, but I have unfortunately not had the opportunity to read his work. I *do* remember him appearing on the television program "Tony Brown's Journal", a Black informational talk show, promoting his book. Since I haven't read the book yet, I'll reserve any comments and/or judgments that I have on it. At the same time, I don't know what his personal agenda is, or his purpose for writing the book, or even who he specifically wrote the book for.

Raise Your Brown Black Fist

I also disagree with his use of the term 'alliance'. An alliance is a temporary partnership between two conflicting groups meant to deal with an immediate threat or issue, eliminating that threat or issue, and then going back to their same old conflicting ways. Coalitions, on the other hand, are long term, and are a means to a common end. I don't see Latinos and African Americans as antagonistic, conflicting groups. We may have our issues with each other, but we're not at each other's throats all of the time. I've witnessed more Black/Brown coalitions than alliances in my life.

I am a staunch Black Nationalist/Pan Africanist/African Internationalist. I am an active and valued member of the Universal Negro Improvement Association (UNIA) here in Virginia (my new home). Yes…the organization still exists. Yes…we still have chapters in the United Snakes, er, I mean, States and abroad. The Black/Brown world is *so* much bigger than just your block or neighborhood. Actually, the Brown world is *a part* of the Black world, considering that 1/3 of Latino roots and culture is derived from Africa. Imagine my surprise when doing some additional research on the UNIA, that we had chapters and divisions located in Latin America? We're more than just an organization; we were to be a functioning government for the unified Black world. The UNIA was located in the following countries in Latin America:

Brazil
Belize (called British Honduras back then)
Colombia
Costa Rica
Cuba
Dominican Republic
Ecuador
Guatemala
Mexico

31

Honduras (my peoples)
Nicaragua
Panama
Puerto Rico
Venezuela

Shocking right? Not really. You see...Black/African descended people exist in those countries. Some of us are here in the U.S., and while you're so busy shooting your mouth off by talking bad about Latinos, you might be insulting one standing right in front of you, or sitting next to you at the job. Really makes you think, doesn't it? Now, whether they're *accepting* of their blackness/African heritage or not...that's a whole 'nother story. Wait...didn't I already cover that?

It's not just the work of my own organization. As I have stated before, you had Latino political organizations that were formed because they were inspired by Black organization that had previously existed. The Young Lords Party and Brown Berets were inspired by the Black Panther Party for Self Defense. These organizations had formed coalitions with each other, and had work together to improve the quality of life in their various communities. To my knowledge, there has been a resurgence of the Brown Berets in recent years, and they have been working closely with regional Black activist organizations. I am unsure if there has been a resurgence of the Young Lords Party, so I cannot comment on that. Also, you have the Latino division of the Nation of Islam. I've known a few of my Latino friends from high school and college that have joined the Nation. As I had stated before in previous articles, the National Council for La Raza was inspired by the NAACP. There's documented history of all of these groups working together at one time, or another. This isn't political pandering, this is the truth. You don't believe me? Get off your ass, and do the research if you want to prove me wrong. It's quite easy to hide behind a computer, and spew trash and taunts behind an online pseudonym. Engaging in a conversation armed with facts to back up whatever it is that you're talking about? That's not as easy as it sounds. I've done my part...several times already. Are you willing to do yours?

Oh, but wait...you want to tell me how that was all back then, and that things are different now. You want to mention about the Latino gangs that are shooting down innocent African Americans on the West Coast. Uh...the criminal element doesn't see color, people... they never have. The only color that they see is green, as in profit. They are nothing more than predators, and we are the prey. They wouldn't care if we were purple with pink polka dots; if they want to rob or shoot at you, they will. And *please* let's not act like African American gang members live by some sort of honor code, and would refuse to terrorize other ethnic groups. They'll attack and terrorize whoever they feel is weak and vulnerable. Gang members prey on *everybody*, even members of their own community/ethnic group. If that weak argument is the best that you can do as a rebuttal...then please don't bother commenting.

I spit facts to people, try to drop some historical relevance as to why things are the way they are today...and all I get back is rhetoric. What's a brother to do?

BLACK VS. BROWN 8: INTERNAL CONFLICT

By: *Kevin Alberto Sabio*

...Un dedicaccion a mi guerrerita revoluccionista...the inspiration for this article...

Much has been said about the conflict between the two communities, not only here on Blacktino.net, but also on various other websites across the country. My own series is dedicated to creating a sense of balance and understanding when it comes to this subject. There is much historical context behind the friction between African Americans and the rising Latino community/ies, with not much of it being initiated by either community. In recent news, much has been made about the rising racial conflicts between the street gangs from both communities, having their conflicts being highlighted in the media as a supreme example of the animosity and strife between the two communities.

My question is....since when in the hell did street gangs become representatives for our communities? So now gang members and convicts are to be looked at as our political representatives? How insulting it that?!

The Black Community

Let's get one thing straight....*neither* community is completely unified in the first place when considering this supposed conflict. It's like I stated before in a number of my earlier articles: integration has helped to fracture the Black community; what do you think its impact would be on Black/Brown relations? For African Americans (or Black people in general), we beef with each other for many superficial reasons: skin color, region, economic status, even nationality. People from the East Coast don't generally like people from the West Coast. New Yorkers don't generally like Bostonians. Brooklynites don't like Harlemites. People from D.C. don't like people from Prince George's County. African Americans beef with people from the Caribbean. I could go on, and on.

I grew up in an immigrant Black community surrounded by people from the Caribbean. They had issues with African Americans, talking very badly about them. At the same time, they had some inter-island beef that they brought with them when they immigrated here to the United States. I witnessed how people got treated differently depending on which island they hailed from. Jamaicans would treat everyone as if they were beneath them. Haitians were treated like unwanted step-children, being disrespected by *all* of the other islanders. The older I got, the more that I saw the friction that existed within the Black community alone. Only when I got into consciousness and activism did I see a change in people's attitudes towards others that were different from them. It wasn't even about sucking up to another person; it was the respect shown to another person who shared my history and culture, and faced the same level of oppression that I faced on a daily basis.

The Latino Community

As far as Latinos are concerned…who ever said that *we* were all unified? In my later school years, I witnessed the friction among the Latino communities in New York, and later when I went away for college. Puerto Ricans and Dominicans didn't get along with each other. Cubans are looked at as arrogant and condescending to other Latinos (well…pre-Marielito Cubans, anyway). Panamanians and Colombians have issues with each other (which I think is more historically based), and even Hondurans and Nicaraguans have their issues with each other. Politically, there is no unifying agenda that brings us all under one umbrella, not even immigration. The rules for immigration don't apply to Cubans, or Puerto Ricans. Puerto Ricans are born citizens of the United States because of their commonwealth status. As for Cubans, they have the "Wet Foot, Dry Foot" policy that only applies to them specifically; if they make it to the U.S. shore without getting caught by the U.S. Coast Guard, they can stay in the country. If they get caught out at sea, they have to return to Cuba. Not to mention how the immigration rules change for them periodically, depending on the administration in the White House. Not to mention, we still have racial issues that we have to contend with within our own community. Afro Latinos still have the issue of (in a sense) gaining acceptance within the 'greater' Latino community.

Conflicted

How can we get along with others, if we can barely get along with ourselves? Our children join gangs, and fight with each other over trivial matters; I was looked at wrong…he wore red, and I wear blue…he stepped on my toe and dirtied my shoe…He's wearing a gold chain, so he thinks he's all that…He's got a nice jacket that I want… so on, and so on. We disrespect each other over stupid, superficial crap. So I don't have a car…big deal? So I'm not making as much money as you…who cares? You have a different skin complexion and hair texture than I do…so what?! So you were raised in the islands and not the U.S…*AND?!?!* So you have a college degree and I don't… whoopty damn do! We need to cut the bullshit, and focus on the true root(s) of our strife and suffering; the lack of resources available to us to allow our communities to flourish.

At least within the Latino community, they do practice nationalism so as to compensate for the lack of resources that are unavailable to them. Alas, It's only practiced in a limited scope, because it usually falls mainly within the boundaries of their particular nationality (Puerto Ricans sell Puerto Rican products to Puerto Ricans; Mexicans sell Mexican products to Mexicans, and so on). Within the African American community, it's done almost on an infinitesimal scale. I *have* seen the rise of Black business networking groups in the last decade and a half, or so…but nothing on the scale like it really could (and should) be. I do remember a bunch of different Black Expos cropping up across the country during the early 90s in many of the major cites that had sizable Black populations. From what I know, their popularity has waned over the years and have either ceased operation, or those expos have become corrupted and commercialized.

Before we start slinging mud and accusations about who's stealing what from whom, let's get *our own* houses in order. Neither group is the bane of the other's existence. We've worked together before in the past, and we can still work together now. The rhetoric from reactionary idiots is only causing us to weaken our forces even more for those who would suffer from us working together as a unified force; the privileged Powers-That-Be. The system that we currently live in was *never* structured for the benefit of People of Color; not unless they chose to act as neo-colonialist gatekeepers to help them maintain the status quo. Even then, there is still a glass ceiling that they can't break through. We need to know who our real enemy is, and take our fight to them. Sun Tzu said it in his famous document *The Art of War*, "The best way to defeat your enemy is to make him/them think that they can't win." Considering the state that our various communities are in...I'd say someone must have been studying really hard....

PART II

BLACK THOUGHTS:
A Political Ideological Perspective for Afro Latinos

By: *Kevin Alberto Sabio*

Many get confused when they hear the following terms being used as far as political ideology is concerned; Black Power/Nationalism, Pan Africanism, Afrocentrism, African Internationalism. Those that are uninitiated may feel that these ideologies are threatening and racist in some way, while others who follow those particular ideologies may feel that they are limiting, or are opposed to each other. In reality, it's all just semantics. They're all interchangeable with each other, and basically call for the same solution; unity, power, and respect for people of African descent. Here on Blacktino.net, I will try to clear up some of the misconceptions about these ideologies, and hope to motivate my fellow Afro Latinos to join the cause. Because of recent conflicts that I've gotten into with online trolls, both on other websites, and here on Blacktino.net, I felt it necessary to delve into this subject, and let it be known how these ideologies impact ALL African descended people.

Some may see Black Power/Nationalism as a strictly African American political manifestation, only concerning itself with African American issues. That is simply untrue. As thoroughly outlined in the Stokely Carmichael/Charles Hamilton book, *"Black Power"*, this stance calls for power to ALL Black People; not just African Americans. Seeing as how Stokely Carmichael/Kwame Toure was of Afro Caribbean descent, I would HIGHLY doubt that he would call for a political ideology that wouldn't encompass or benefit people of his own national/regional background. That work was followed up by the ancestor Dr. Amos Wilson in his seminal work, *"Blueprint for Black Power"*. In this heavily detailed dossier (almost 900 pages), He goes in-depth with his analysis of Black Power as a viable political concept, and the steps needed to be taken to make Black Power a reality and living entity. Wilson breaks down what power is, how it can be used (and misused), and how people can obtain power politically, economically, culturally, educationally, physically, and even spiritually to a certain extent. Demographically speaking, the African population in the United States (in total) has the size and capacity to become it's own self-sustaining nation-state, and would only be able to survive in the long run unless it begins to see itself as a nation within a nation. The African descended population in America can be seen as a catalyst for a strong nation state and provide empowerment, not only for themselves, but for a unified African Diaspora in both the political arena and economically.

This leads me to Pan Africanism. The greatest example of Pan Africanism was the work of the honorable Marcus Mosiah Garvey, and his Universal Negro Improvement Association. Having traveled across the globe at a young age, Garvey saw how Africans/African Descendants were treated throughout the world. We were continuously on the bottom of the social ladder, and were suffering socially, economically, and politically. Garvey created the very first chapter of the UNIA in 1914 in his home country of

Jamaica. The organization was to be a fully functioning government made to represent for all African peoples across the world. Chapters and divisions were set up ALL OVER the globe throughout the Caribbean, the United States, on the continent of Africa herself, and even in LATIN AMERICA. Even after his (illegal) expulsion and deportation from the United States, Garvey still had an impact, influencing many of the continental African leaders who were to one day govern their countries into independence, such as Kwame Nkrumah, Sekou Toure, Jomo Kenyatta, and Julius Nyererre. His work and ideology is thoroughly outlined in the books *"Race First"*, written by Tony Martin, and also *"The Philosophy and Opinions of Marcus Garvey, Vol. I-III"*, edited by Amy Jacques Garvey. Dr. Wilson even covers Garvey and his work in his own book, citing the economic and political successes of the UNIA, and the blueprint that was left for a means of international trade and commerce throughout the African Diaspora.

Afrocentrism has been considered the most controversial of these ideologies, considering that it takes on the system that we live in head on. It has caused many debates and mudslinging in academic circles, with the mainstream institutions denouncing it, not only in academia, but also on their campuses. In his seminal work *"Afrocentricity"*, Dr. Molefe K. Asante outlines what Afrocentrism is, and why it's necessary. The only thing that causes Afrocentrism to be considered controversial (at least to the Powers that Be and their neo-colonialist supporters) is the primacy of Africa in its ideology. All things African are considered primary in thought, culture, education, and mode of living. We are not taught about our history and/or culture in mainstream society, or in the mainstream educational system. To go against the status quo is almost considered blasphemy, and makes one into an outcast unless you conform in the end. Why not be free to embrace this part of our history and culture? Why should we be denied a part of ourselves just to fit into the so-called mainstream?

As it is, we exist in an oppressive, white supremacist system. We are still suffering the effects of colonialism and slavery. Think I'm wrong? Ask yourselves these questions, as posed by Dr. Wilson about the affects of slavery and colonialism on society today:

What language do you speak in?
What clothes do you wear?
What religion/spiritual belief do you practice?
What foods do you eat?
Is this what your ancestors were doing in the past, or were any of these imposed on them?

Makes you think for a second, doesn't it? There are a few other authors that I could recommend concerning the ideology of Afrocentrism, but my library is inaccessible to me at the time of this writing, so I am unable to give you the titles. I would suggest researching certain authors and scholars such as Dr. Na'im Akbar, Haki Matubhuti, Dr. Maulana Karenga, Dr. Jawanzaa Kunjufu, Dr. Marcia Sutherland, Wilson Jeremiah Moses, Ivan Van Sertima, Runoko Rashidi, Thomas Parham, Cyrus H. Gordon, and Robin Walker.

Afro Latinos

Now after having gone through all of that…what does any of this have to do with Afro Latinos? Everything. They are Africans, whether they admit it or not. This is not to impose any political belief on them, it's just fact. Don't believe me? Do some historical research. One of my favorites is researching the work of Dr. Eric Williams in his titles, "*The Negro in the Caribbean*", and "*Documents of West Indian History*". You can also try Richard Price's "*Maroon Societies*", as he discusses those Africans who were forcefully brought to these shores, and were able to escape from their enslavement, and create their own societies. The story of Yanga from Mexico comes to mind, as well as the Maroons from Jamaica lead by Queen Nanny. You also have the work of Dr. Arlene Torres in her book titled, *"Blackness in Latin American and the Caribbean"*. There's also other research available, such as Patrick J. Carroll's, *"Blacks in Colonial Vera Cruz"*, Benga-In Nunez's, *"Dictionary of Afro-Latin American Civilization"*, Minority Rights Group's, *"No Longer Invisible: Afro-Latin Americans Today"*, or Pedro Perez Sarduy's, *"Afro-Cuba Voices: On Race and Identity in Contemporary Cuba"*. I would also encourage the reading of articles written by such writers as Carlos Cooks, Karen Juanita Carrillo, and the works of Prof. Victor Vega, and Dr. Marta Moreno-Vega. There are also other websites to peruse to get more information about Afro Latinos and our connections to the African Diaspora, such as AfroCubaWeb.com, Afropresencia.com, and AfroLatinoproject.org. With the jacking of ancestral Afro Latino lands by the respective Latin American governments, our unity within the African Diaspora is not only necessary, but essential. We cannot survive solely on our own. We are a part of the unified Black/African World.

Of course, according to my troll on Blacktino.net, I have my head up my ass, so what do I know? I guess the works by the authors mentioned above negates EVERYTHING that's supposedly known about this subject, the world according to him. But supposedly, he's an expert, and I'm just a peon with a bit mouth. Of course, there are so many other scholars and activists, and other works that I could mention to refute this Internet Tough Guy, but I think that this article would suffice. Besides, that would take too long, and I have better things to do. I don't call myself an activist for nothing.

Uhuru Sase, Y paz.

BLACK THOUGHTS:
A Political Ideological Perspective for Afro Latinos
Part II: Ways(s) of the Black Fist

By: *Kevin Alberto Sabio*

A mi guerrerita revoluccionista....you'll never be alone in the struggle, not if I have anything to say about it....

In a person's life, there are many instances that shape our being, and take us on a particular course in our lives. For some, it might be something that they've always had ingrained in them from birth, while for others it might be some sort of chance encounter with a particular person or event/experience to motivate them to travel down this path towards enlightenment and activism that they were seemingly destined to take. I never envisioned myself to be a voice of/for the people; merely another souljah fighting for the cause...a whole hearted believer just trying to do my part. Blacktino.net has allowed me this opportunity to be a voice for the voiceless, with me not initially realizing how far reaching my words can be and have been. Now knowing better, I plan to take this responsibility a lot more seriously.

About a decade ago, during the height of the so-called 'Latin Explosion', a comment was made about Latinos having surpassed, or about to surpass, African Americans as the new 'majority' minority here in the United States. A big stink was made about it in certain segments of the Black press, making it seem as if this was such a big travesty and calamity. The brothers and sisters who traveled within my social political circle gave a uniformed shrug and stated, "Well... so what? What has that status ever gotten *us*?" I had previously talked about this experience in my previous article series entitled "Black vs. Brown", in which I tried to put the friction between the two communities in its proper historical and political perspective. Being a Latino of African descent (and VERY proud of it), it was felt that I would be able to provide a unique perspective to this situation. I caught the ignorance and animosity of it from both sides. I heard a lot of ignorance and racial animosity fly out the mouths of members of the Black community. At the same time, as a Latino of African descent, I was never fully accepted by Latinos, specifically if they were racist against Black people. It was a constant battle that I had to wage; battling the ignorance and stupidity of members from both communities. In "Black vs. Brown", I talked about the many causes of these issues between our people, with many of them being deeply rooted in our collective histories. This time around...I want to be more solution oriented.

As far as Latinos being the new 'majority' minority in the country, where does that place someone like me? I'm not fully accepted by the 'greater' Latino community, nor are Afro Latinos in general. Our existence is denied to a certain extent. To be accepted into the 'greater' Latino community, we would have to assimilate, and deny much of our African heritage just to fit in. Hmm...why does this sound so familiar? I've suffered from prejudice and racism from 'my own', with examples too numerous to list here. Yet, this isn't about bashing anyone; it's about accepting and learning about who you are.

One third of Latino culture is derived from Africa. Slaves were transported from the continent to the 'New World' to provide labor for European colonists/imperialists for their own personal enrichment, and that of their mother country. The Africans were brought in when the numbers of the indigenous people who originally inhabited these lands were either being wiped out by war with, or diseases brought by, the colonizers/imperialists. As an extension of the Slave Trade, it soon moved northward to what is now known as North America, with a part of the continent becoming what we now know today as the United States. Slavery was brutal in both regions, as it was throughout this entire hemisphere. Our ancestors suffered greatly at the hands of their oppressors and captors. But, unlike what we're taught in the 'mainstream' educational system, our ancestors didn't take their enslavement lying down. Many did fight back. Throughout Latin America and the Caribbean, there were those that fought and escaped to freedom, and formed their own free and independent societies. These ancestors were most commonly known as the Maroons. You also have those in North America that fought for their freedom. Everyone has heard about the warrior queen Harriet Tubman and the Underground Railroad, but how many of us have ever heard of the Black Seminoles out of what is now Florida? They fought three wars against the United States government, beating them back TWICE. There were also the many slave rebellions, like the Stono Rebellion in South Carolina in 1739. We should also mention our diasporic ancestors such as Yanga from Mexico, Carlota from Cuba, and Sebastian Lemba and Touissant L'oveture from what's now known as the Dominican Republic and Haiti respectively.

There is much that we can learn from each other. To a certain extent, those Africans from Latin American were able to retain more of their cultural heritage from the mother continent than those of their brethren that were sent to what eventually became the United States. It's evident from those of us that are practitioners of Santeria, Lucumi, or Candombe; all believed to be sub sects or variations of the Yoruba faith. Drumming is still a part of Afro Latino culture, as well as certain African-based styles of dance and fighting arts that are taught and passed down from generation to generation. There is also much that we have learned from our northern brothers and sisters. We've learned from our fiery revolutionaries to be proud and accepting of our African roots and features. We've learned about organizing and mobilizing ourselves to fight for our rights as a people. We've learned that we are not alone in our struggle, and that there are those that we can call on to help us in our time of need…especially in this day and time, with many Afro Latino ancestral lands being taken from them by their respective national governments.

I had gotten into an online spat a few months ago on another networking site, with the site being dedicated to authors of African descent. The forum posted on this site was about dedicating May as 'Latino Book Month', celebrating the achievements of Latino writers on the site. One particular troll had to post a negative reply, being highly disrespectful towards Latinos, and our history. This situation was quite sad and comical; sad because this person chose to expose his ignorance and prejudice towards a people that he obviously knows nothing about, and comical because of the fact that, this person was contradicting his online handle that was supposed to connote his high level of (supposed) intelligence, and his responses in our argument were written so atrociously that a third grader would have been embarrassed by his writing skills…and this person is a published author! Quite obviously, he was an idiot suffering from ITGS (Internet Tough Guy/Gal Syndrome), and he was thoroughly trashed. The site creator was thankful for my responses, having been quite upset with this poster's comments. We're not so far apart as others would want to make it seem. We are kindred spirits, brethren, long-lost cousins. We are a part of each other, connected on a deeper level, spiritually and culturally. You have suffered as I have suffered; have had blood shed as we have had blood shed. Let us share our pain and experiences, and take this to the next level.

To be continued.....

BLACK THOUGHTS:
A Political Ideological Perspective
for Afro Latinos
Part III: Reflections of Me

By: *Kevin Alberto Sabio*

I have to admit...I hated the 'Latin Explosion' when it came about around ten years ago. I had previously touched on this subject here on Blacktino.net before, but I now want to go a little further in-depth about it. I found it quite insulting on several different levels. For one thing, Latinos have been around in the entertainment field in this country for a few generations now; to act as if we're *just* coming onto the scene is disrespectful and insulting. You had the Salsa bands and Latin Jazz bands touring the country during the early and mid parts of this past century. You had musicians such as Carlos Santana and Jerry Garcia making an impact in Rock music during the 60s and 70s. Also, you had Latin Freestyle music (which I'm a huge fan of) in the 80s and 90s, along with other Pop Music artists such as Gloria Estefan, Lisa Lisa & Cult Jam, and Sheila E. We had been doing our thing in the music and movie industry for a good while now; we didn't just arrive on the scene out of the blue.

The other thing that I hated about the 'Latin Explosion' and found insulting...? I never saw myself being represented by the people behind the hype machine, or anyone that looked anything like me. As far as Afro Latinos were concerned...we didn't exist. Latinos were shown as light, bright...and damn near white.

There were a few notable exceptions to this 'rule' during the whole 'Latin Explosion'. You saw a few Afro Latina beauty queens picked to represent their respective countries, specifically Miss Colombia and Miss Honduras. But for the most part, Afro Latinos were relegated to the status of *persona non grata*. You never saw us during the whole 'Explosion', not unless you dug around really deep in the underground circles. While we were being bombarded with images of Ricky Martin, Enrique Iglesias, Mark Anthony, and Jennifer Lopez... you hardly got the opportunity to see or hear groups or artists such as DLG (Dark Latin Groove), Proyecto Uno, Fulanito, or El General (a precursor to the current Reggeton movement) in the mainstream. I couldn't see a wonderful talent like Lisette Melendez, but got to see and hear plenty of a (now blonde) Shakira. I could hear Rock En Espanol, but would be hard pressed to find R&B music performed by artists like Son By 4, Veronica, or other artists associated with labels like H.O.L.A Recordings, or Sir George Entertainment. Gee, I wonder why?

I'm reminded of a comedy routine performed by Puerto Rican comedian Herb Quinones. He reflects on his up bringing, and how he was taught by his family that, "You're not Black...you're Puerto Rican!" despite his obvious African features. For much of his life, he believed what he was told (being taught that his nationality was his race), and would fight anyone that would tell him otherwise. In his routine, he states that the NYPD cleared up that racial distinction for him during a profiling incident in his youth. He was riding around with some friends in a car, when they ended up getting pulled over. The routine goes like this:

NYPD: *All you n*ggers get out of the car!*

HQ: *My friends got out...I didn't move.*

NYPD: (angrily approaches car) *I SAID...all you n*ggers get out of the car!*

HQ: (adamantly) *I'm NOT black...I'm Puerto Rican!*

NYPD: (roughly hauls him out of car) *Man...you're just a SPANISH n*gger!*

A pretty telling experience, right? Yet, as funny as Herb is, you'll never see or hear Latino comedians like him, or Ruperto Vanderpool in mainstream Latino comedy specials. Being from New York, I was lucky to hear about comedians like them on the underground comedy scene out there, along with a very funny J.J. Ramirez.

Aside from the music industry, we hardly get represented on television, or in the movies. When was the last time you saw a T.V. show that revolved around an Afro Latino family? We've made some inroads as far as overall representation, but Afro Latinos are still nonexistent. When she was younger, my niece used to love to watch the television show "Taina" on Nickelodeon, starring the very talented Christina Vidal. At the same time, you had the series "The Garcia Brothers", also on Nickelodeon at the time. You also had shows on cable like "Resurrection Boulevard" and "My American Family" on PBS. Again...this was great as far as having a Latino presence on television was concerned, but where were WE in all of this? It's rare for an Afro Latino to be cast in a Latino role in film or television. We normally get relegated to playing only African American/Black roles. Look at the careers of actors such as Zoe Saldana, Merlin Santana (R.I.P), Tatyana Ali, Alfonso Ribeiro, Gina Torres, and Christina Milian. Very few Afro Latino actors are able to be cast consistently in a 'Latino' role because of how they look. The few exceptions would probably be Dania Ramirez, Lauren Velez, Wanda De Jesus, and Rick Gonzalez. Also, when was the last time you saw a movie that's subject matter was about Afro Latinos? You might have to sift through many independently made movies on the underground scene.

I know that with the African Diaspora Film Festival, an independent Black film festival based out of New York City (www.nyadff.org), they have a program dedicated to films made by, or whose subject matter is about, Latinos of African descent. It's through there that I learned about Afro Latino filmmakers such as Gloria Rolando, Sergio Giral, Tomas Gutierrez, and Sara Gomez, all from Cuba. Only through certain underground independent Latino macrocinema networks back in New York did I see us as a people being reflected in all of our various shades and colors, like La Cinema Café, Chica Luna, and LatinBeat. Much of it is being lead by Dominican/Dominican American and Puerto Rican filmmakers based out of the Washington Heights and East Harlem sections of Manhattan. Many of these films can be seen in the various independent film festivals based in New York other than ADFF, such as Urbanworld Film Festival, the New York International Latino Film Festival, ImageNation Film and Music Festival, and Reel Sisters of the Diaspora Film Festival to name a few. Even though you have to search for it, our stories are being told, and are out there.

Much of this motivates me to work on (and continue with) my own cinematic projects. I have a few cinematic and animated television projects in the vault as I write this, and looking to get produced in the near future. There needs to be a truer representation of who we are. Our stories need to be, and will be, told.

BLACK THOUGHTS:
A Political Ideological Perspective for Afro Latinos
Part IV: Voice of the Voiceless

By: *Kevin Alberto Sabio*

I had recently gone out to a Latino heritage festival out here in my new home state of Virginia. Being that this is Latino/Hispanic Heritage Month, I had decided to come out and represent my Honduran heritage at this festival; one of the few opportunities that I have to *not* be the quintessential 'angry black male', and get to relax and let my hair down, so to speak. I wore my paraphernalia (hat and wristbands) promoting my Honduran heritage, even buying a jersey with the Honduran flag on it at the festival when I finally arrived. The festival itself was quite nice; not really being on the scale that I'm used to being from New York, but it was still entertaining and enjoyable. The only downer was getting asked the same stupid question from those who dared to ask...

Are you really from Honduras?

No...I'm wearing all of this blue-and-white because it brings out the color of my eyes...

It was quite troubling for me to experience this (yet again). Another Latino festival has come and gone…and yet another missed opportunity for Latinos' African roots to be shown and celebrated. It was funny because even the vendor who had sold me the jersey (who *also* happened to be Honduran) questioned me as to where I was from. Many assumed that I was African American, and was wearing the stuff just to fit in at the festival. I do remember receiving a few dirty looks from a few Indigenous-looking Latinos at the festival. Being the Brooklyn native that I am, I mean-mugged them back, letting them know that I wasn't intimidated by them. I'm not some interloper trying to crash 'their' festival. I belonged at that festival just as much as they did. Later that weekend, I had called a friend from back home to tell her about my experiences. She was proud of me for going, and felt that my presence at that festival was much needed, despite my reservations and experiences after the fact. Now looking back on it…I agree with her.

The Internet

Afro Latinos are rarely seen, and never heard. Even at Latino cultural celebrations, our voices and experiences are seldom heard. The mainstream media, Latino or otherwise, doesn't provide us with any representation at all. In order for us to have our voices heard we pretty much have to do for self. In recent years, there have been a number of publications, albeit online publications, that have sprouted up and are providing an outlet for issues affecting Afro Latinos to be heard. They speak on our political issues, explore our various cultures, and some even provide news from the respective countries that we come from. Some have even become interactive, providing streaming videos or audio podcasts. Many of these sites have been started and are run by activists, journalists, and scholars who are heavily involved in Afro Latino affairs. Were it not for these brave souls, who is to say that these outlets would ever exist otherwise?

There are several sites out there for you to choose from, depending on what it is that you want to know. Sites such as AfroCubaWeb.com, Afrocolombians.com, and Afrovenezuelanos.com are more culture-specific, dealing with issues affecting the African population of those respective countries. Other sites such as VidaAfroLatina.com, AfroLatin@Project.org, and Afropresencia.com are more universal in their approach, dealing with issues that affect Afro Latinos in general. Sites like these also have links to other Afro Latino websites and organizations. Though some of these sites might be written in Spanish, certain sites do carry a bilingual feature, allowing their content to be translated into English if your literacy in Spanish isn't very up to par.

Music

Now, more than ever, there seems to be a new level of racial consciousness rising up from Afro Latinos, specifically from the younger generation. You may hear some deep political thoughts being broadcasted by artists such as Immortal Technique, a Hip Hop MC, or Tego Calderon, a popular Reggeton artist. I remember in my younger days listening to Hip Hop artists/groups such as the Orishas from Cuba, or the Arsonists who were based out of my hometown of New York. You also have independent artists out there speaking on their roots, or expressing political thoughts in their music, such as Viva Fidel based out of Milwaukee, or Willie Villainova and Rebel Diaz from New York City. There are probably many more that I can't name at this time, only because I have yet to know of them. The elder Salseros, Merengueros, and Latin Jazz musicians started it back in the 'old country'; it's now time for the next generation to pick up the baton, and carry on.

And lastly, there's me. I don't claim to be any type of leader or mouthpiece, but I will do what I can to let others know about our issues, and that we exist. There is much ignorance that needs to be combated from Black and Brown alike. There is limited acceptance, if any, from within 'mainstream' Latino culture and society. Race is still considered a taboo subject; sometimes considered specifically an 'American' issue. That couldn't be further from the truth. At the same time, I have also butted heads with, not just regular African Americans, but with so-called 'conscious' revolutionaries within the Black Community. The ignorance is abundant, and the silence is deafening. It's time for our voices to be heard. Now, SCREAM!!!!!!

Black Thoughts:
A Political Ideological Perspective
for Afro Latinos
Part V: Politics & Bullsh*t

By: *Kevin Alberto Sabio*

It's election season…time to get your vote on!

I had recently gotten into a situation with an associate of mine that left me a bit disturbed. This associate had sent me several emails soliciting my help in a grassroots campaign to help support Sen. Barak Obama's Democratic candidacy for president. After being annoyed with the numerous emails that this person had sent me, I finally replied that I was planning on supporting the Cynthia McKinney-Rosa Clemente campaign, considering that I've followed both women's political careers for some time now, and feel that they are more viable candidates as far as my political interests are concerned. This associate replied back that, "I hope that your vote isn't wasted, and McCain ends up winning."

WHAT?!?!?! Huh?!?!?!

Since when is having an alternative political voice a bad thing? Considering that this person is supposed to be a member of the "conscious" community, that response really bothered me. From what I know about former Congresswoman McKinney and Ms. Clemente, they both have a proven track record of fighting for their communities and constituents respectively. What has Senator Obama done for our community other than being born half Kenyan?

Especially in this day and time when there is a supposed rift between the Black and Latino communities, the candidacy of the McKinney-Clemente team is unprecedented, and should be receiving more press and attention in our communities. You have two women of color running for the highest office of this country! After hearing all of the hoopla being made about Senator Clinton's Democratic candidacy, and now Gov. Sarah Palin's nomination as Republican John McCain's running mate, all of this rhetoric about the rise of feminist politics...you would think that a team of TWO women on the same ticket would be having a huge political impact on this year's political race. Or, is it that you have to be the right *kind* of woman (white) to get that type of media attention? Cynthia McKinney is no lightweight; her record speaks for itself. Rosa Clemente has been active in the community for years, from her college days on. What I really respect about former Congresswoman McKinney is her outreach to the Afro Latino communities being affected by the land-grabbing of their respective governments of their ancestral lands.

Of course, this is not the first time that Blacks and Latinos have worked together politically. During my time in New York City, you would hear plenty about the efforts of the Black and Puerto Rican Caucus, fighting for legislation for their respective communities. Also, the efforts of many grassroots political organizations can be noted, both contemporarily and historically. Rosa Clemente's membership in the Malcolm X Grassroots Movement, and all of her activity with the organization and outreach to the Hip Hop community, is a testament to that. I also remember hearing about the efforts of groups such as 100 Blacks in Law Enforcement and the Latino

Officers Association, both law enforcement fraternal organizations, doing much to fight for the community. You also have the Latino contingent of the Nation of Islam doing much to help to uplift the community, and spread the influence of Islam.

Historically speaking, you have the influence of the Universal Negro Improvement Association (UNIA) throughout Latin America. They had SEVERAL divisions and chapters overseas, probably THE largest Black Nationalist organization to ever exist. They were located in several countries, including Honduras, Cuba, Dominican Republic, Costa Rica, Puerto Rico, Colombia, Panama, Mexico, and several others. Also, you had the influence of the Black Panther Party for Self Defense, and how they helped inspire the formation of both the Young Lords Party and Brown Berets. In recent years, there has been a resurgence of the Brown Berets in the American southwest, working locally with grassroots Black community organizations. There is also the influence of the NAACP on the National Council for La Raza, sometimes seen as the Latino/Chicano version of the NAACP. The two organizations have actually worked together in the recent past on several campaigns over the years.

Also, for me, is Sister Rosa Clemente herself. She is a proud Afro Boricua, proudly proclaiming her African roots and ancestry, and a strong advocate for Afro Latino rights and culture. Because of her activism, she has a lot of experience with the impact of American foreign policy on other countries, especially those policies affecting our closest neighbors in Latin America. She is a fearless and tireless worker and fighter, as is her running-mate, and would work hard to improve our relations in the region. If my work schedule at the time permitted it, I would try to catch her radio program on WBAI-FM with her on-air co-host Sally O'Brien.

So, come Election Day this November, I know who I will be casting my vote for. This is not to disrespect the candidacy of Sen. Obama, but why consider his campaign as a new precedent in

American politics, and not the McKinney-Clemente candidacy? Two highly qualified women of color running for the highest office of this country, and it's *not* considered groundbreaking? Why should Sen. Obama be looked at as a messiah, and the McKinney-Clemente ticket as pariahs? We have a lot of good orators in the Black community; we see them every Sunday (and sometimes daily on the street corners). If you truly want change, then this is it. I won't put ALL of my faith in electoral politics to effect change; that can only come from within. But, casting my vote for a team that I truly believe in…that's a real start to effecting change. My vote won't be wasted.

BLACK THOUGHTS:
A Political Ideological Perspective for Afro Latinos
Part VI: Word Power

By: *Kevin Alberto Sabio*

People understand very little about the power of words...

I remember one incident in my youth, during my late teens/early twenties, when I was hanging out with some friends of mine (at the time) from high school, in which I was supposed to be forming a musical group with (they were to be the singers in the group, and I was to be the emcee). We were having a conversation one time about group matters when one of my friends/groupmates replied in a jovial fashion, "I'm a Spic, and proud of it." His response caused me to raise a surprised eyebrow at him, considering that I was the angry militant of the group. In response, he dared me to ask him why he would refer to himself in such a manner. After a few seconds of contemplation, I bit.

"Okay...*why* are you proud to be a Spic?"

"...Because we're Spanish People In Control! Get it?"

I have to admit that at the time I laughed at his response, thinking that it was on the clever side; taking a word of negative connotation, and turning it into a positive. As the emcee of the group (and secondary song writer), I had actually penned a few songs (actually two; the original song with rhyme verse, and the rap remix) in response to his witty acronym, turning it into our political statement. Since I was the radical of the group, I had always tried to express my political beliefs through my art, using it as a tool to 'edutain' the masses. It's been many moons since I've even *thought* about picking up the mic; it just wasn't in me to be an emcee. It's been even longer since I had a falling out with my ex-groupmates/former friends to do the music thing, and revolutionize the music industry and the masses. But…that particular memory has always stuck with me.

It reminds me of some brothers and sisters that I deal with in the 'conscious community', specifically those of us from the Hip Hop generation. I knew a few who would try to break down the word 'nigga' into an acronym to mean something positive. I remember Tupac's take on the word, using 'Never Ignorant, Getting Goals Accomplished' as a way to break down what the word means, lessening its negative power. I also remember hearing another breakdown of the word to mean 'Nubianism Is a God Given Achievement'. There were quite a few other catchy acronyms that were used, that I can't remember at this time. As I get older, I wonder if any of it makes any sense at all. The N-word is overused so pervasively in modern-day mainstream Rap music that it makes you wonder if anybody even really cares anymore?

I remember that when I had first gotten into Black consciousness and activism in my mid teens (sixteen, actually), I had simply refused to use the word. During my early college days, I went a stretch of two years of totally omitting the word from my vocabulary. I took pride in the fact that I had the discipline to go that long without using the N-word to address another brother or sister. Being from New York

City, we had so many ways of greeting each other, there was actually *no need* to use that word to address one another. Of course, there were times when people would get on my bad side, and I would curse them out, and call and/or refer to them as the N-word in a fit of anger. As I get older, I have relaxed from that stance a bit, as far as totally omitting the word from my vocabulary. Hey...some of us *do* act like that, and need to be called out accordingly. At the same time, I'm learning more and more about how the power of words can have such an impact on a person, whether positively or negatively.

I remember watching a scene from the movie "Remember the Titans". The now-integrated team went off to camp to train, and the two groups of students had to learn how to get along with each other and the new coaching staff. After a few racial fights, the coach (played by Denzel Washington) forced the team into a long run as a form of discipline for fighting. There was a particular scene between two of the players; one White, one Black (played by Wood Harris). The White player was chiding the Black player for acting in a selfish manner, despite probably being the best player on the team athletically. His response to this confrontation will forever be etched into my brain:

Black Player: "You're the captain of the team, right?"

White Player: "Yeah, that right..."

Black Player: "You think that I have a bad attitude, right?"

White Player: "Yep, yes I do! That's exactly what I'm saying!"

Black Player: "*Attitude* reflects *leadership...Captain!*"

Needless to say, the White Player was stunned by his response, and really had to reflect on what was said. In the beginning of the movie, his character would only have criticized the Black players, but none of the whites that he knew. After that encounter, the character changed his tune, and started be a team leader for the *entire* team. That line had also made a big impact on me as well. It makes me more aware of my own words and deeds; seeing if I'm living up to the high revolutionary standards that I tend to speak often about.

Another experience that left an impression on me happened earlier this year at a function that the members of my organization threw (the UNIA). It was an anniversary benefit dinner celebrating my division's 10th anniversary in operation. We had another member of the organization come in to be our keynote speaker at the event (who now holds office as the President General of the entire UNIA). He gave a very powerful presentation, not only addressing the history of our organization and the legacy of our founder Marcus Mosiah Garvey, but also things that we have yet to achieve as an organization, and as a people. Having constantly gotten into debates and arguments with other so-called conscious people, he said something that I thought and felt were very profound:

"The more you know, the more you know DON'T know."

Basically, it's all a learning process. We're all *still* learning, and NOBODY has *all* of the answers. Luckily for me, I videotaped the event, so I can pop in the DVD that I made of his speech if I ever need some motivation to combat any battle fatigue that I'm feeling.

It's not just the words that are spoken. What motivated me to embrace nationalism and race consciousness was reading these two works; "Autobiography of Malcolm X" by Alex Haley, and "Souls on Ice" by Eldridge Cleaver. Those two seminal works forever transformed me, and my initial way of thinking. They were just the start to many other classic and contemporary works that I've absorbed over the years. There are still many more works that I'm looking forward to getting my hands on. I still have yet to bring down the rest of my personal library from my old residence to my new place.

And lastly, there is the impact that my own words have had on many others, seen and unseen. When I (recently) got into writing online commentaries, I had *no idea* what type of impact my words would have on others. I was simply amazed to see my work spread all over cyberspace, and how some people held my work in such high regard. I have a comrade of mine who allowed me to repost my articles on his networking site (in which he reposted them elsewhere as well), and the responses to them were so immense that some of *his* comrades had them translated into other languages, and reposted elsewhere as well! I was shocked and surprised to hear how much of an impact my words were having on others. It's not that I don't have faith in my writing skills; far from it. It's really *how* these people are moved and motivated by what I said. I have always received accolades for my entertainment works, so praise for my pieces really comes as no surprise; trying to get them produced, though, is another battle all together, and is another discussion for another day.

With that said, we discover that Word Power is indeed a *very* powerful force. And as was stated in the origin of the comic book character Spider-Man, "With great power, comes great responsibility".

Nuff said.

BLACK THOUGHTS:
A Political Ideological Perspective for Afro Latinos
Part VII: Heart of a Souljahr

By: *Kevin Alberto Sabio*

"I do what I love, love what I do
Doing this for me, as well as for you
Say true if the words that I'm speaking you people feel (true!),
Who in your opinion is really keeping it real?"
- Substantial, rap artist; "What I Love", © 2006

I'm unapologetic in what I believe in. I'm a diehard Nationalist/
Pan Africanist/Afrocentrist. That has gotten me into a lot of trouble
over the years, specifically when it comes to my activism. There have
been times when people have vigorously disagreed with me, who
have professed to believe the same ideological principles that I do.
There have been many times when I have been let down by people
who I thought were true comrades. The most recent spat was this
past election season here in the United States. I've seen many battles
lines drawn, and some even crossed, because of the pre-election lead-

up activity, and the post-election results. We now seem even more fractured a community than we were even beforehand; Reformists/ Integrationists on the one side, and radical Revolutionaries on the other. Friendships have been strained, and loyalties have now been called into question.

Bottom line…tough. I won't apologize. Why should I?

In the end, all that we have are our principles. If you choose to compromise them, then why should we even bother to speak on ANY issues concerning change for our community/people? I'm not going to compromise what I believe in just for personal advancement, or just to fit in. I wasn't raised that way, nor am I built that way. There've been many times where I ended up as the outsider and the outcast because I chose to stand up for what I believed in. That was pretty much my experience as a student activist. To this day, I still don't regret any of the decisions that I made back then. I'm fighting for what I believe in its purest and most unadulterated form.

There are many who have dismissed those of us in the Pan-Africanist/Black Nationalist/Afrocentrist community for what we believe, and what we have been doing (and already done) in the community. We tend to get dismissed for what we do, yet if some commercial personality or politician does a watered down version of what we do (or have done), it's considered cutting edge, and progressive. If we tend to criticize said commercial personality or politician for it, we get labeled as being "jealous", or "haters". It reminds me of the same issue that some of my associates in the arts have to deal with, like some of these overnight commercial sensations in the music industry (most likely created BY the industry) getting all of the attention while they continue to toil in the underground, or those filmmakers that are struggling on the Black film festival circuit, while some terrible films out of Hollywood are getting distributed through major channels. It's disrespectful, and quite insulting; you do all of the groundwork, but don't get anywhere near the accolades, or the same level of respect nor support that's deserved for not being 'socially acceptable', or 'commercially viable' by the mainstream of society. Such is the life for activists. Then again, we don't do what we do to be popular; we do it because it's needed.

I've had many battles with nonbelievers and half-steppers, especially during my college days. There were times when my own organizational members sabotaged my attempts to institute certain programs or events on campus, or form a coalition with other student organizations trying to bring some sort of change on campus on our behalf. I'd faced threats of expulsion a number of times during my college days, getting kicked out of the dorms twice for my defiance. People thought that I was crazy for the way that I carried myself. I'm not crazy, nor am I a zealot; I'm a true believer. There were those who felt that the likes of the UNIA, Black Panther Party for Self Defense, Young Lords Party, and Brown Berets were crazy. There was a lot that they had done for our people and our communities that they don't get the proper credit for. The Free Lunch program wasn't started by the government; that was the creation of the Black Panthers. The Young Lords Party had taken a van with some medical supplies, and started testing the people in the community for lead and sickle cell. The UNIA had created many businesses, owned property (domestically and abroad), and instituted many programs of self reliance and nationalism on a global scale.

The new buzz word of the day is 'change'. How can you expect change, but yet you still want to practice the same old methodology that hasn't worked yet? This country won't change no matter *who* is in office. The change that is needed needs to come from the *self*... *not* some politician, or the government. Consciousness is an ever evolving process, and I'm continuing to refine my craft. It was stated that, with the results of the recent election, that the old revolutionary paradigm is now outdated and has become obsolete, and that now a new political paradigm has been created. That's CRAP! When have we *ever* practiced Black Nationalism or Pan Africanism *en masse?* The answer is never. How can that ideological process be obsolete and ineffective if we've never tried to practice it *as a whole?!* We've been so conditioned and ingrained with this integrationist/assimilationist ideological belief for so long, that we've deluded ourselves into believing that there is *no other* alternative political recourse available to us. The system that we live in doesn't need to be reformed…it needs to be created anew. To quote Chuck D from Public Enemy, "Neither party is mine…not the jackass, or the elephant!"

When I reached the voting aged, I registered as an Independent. I didn't want to be tied down to any political party; I wanted to be free to choose to support who I wanted to support during election time. In this respect, I continue to follow the ideological thinking of other radical revolutionaries that have come before me, believing that we should form *our own* political party(ies) or voting blocks, and have the major political parties fight for our vote. As it is, the Republican and the Democratic parties are nothing more than two sides of the same coin. *Neither* party has our best interest at heart. One takes us for granted (Democrats), while the other completely ignores us (Republicans). At least with the Republicans, they are more honest in their dislike/disrespect for us. The Democrats just put a kinder face on our oppression. And for those of you who consider the Republicans to be the Evil Empire…the Republicans of today are nothing more than the Dixiecrats of old. Not much has changed, and playing the same old tired games haven't done us much good. We're still no better off now, than we were before. The Two-party system that currently exists in this country is a joke, and we need to have other alternative political voices (and choices) be heard.

People want to use the results of the recent election as an example of our collective power. That is NOTHING compared to what we could *really* accomplish on a global scale if we really put our collective minds to it. Such examples have been cited in the works of great thinkers/scholars such as Dr. Amos Wilson in his phenomenal work *"Blueprint for Black Power"*, Cheik Anta Diop in his work *"Black Africa: The Economic and Cultural Basis for a Federated State"*, Dr. Chancellor Williams in *"The Rebirth of African Civilization"*, and Ezrah Aharone in his works *"Pawned Sovereignty"*, and his recent follow-up *"Sovereign Evolution"*. I also can't leave out the works of John Henrik Clarke, specifically *"Pan Africanism or Perish"*, or all three volumes of *"The Philosophy and Opinions of Marcus Garvey"* written by his wife Amy Jacques Garvey. Instead of just viewing these books as just enlightened reading and intellectual theory, we NEED to be putting the theory behind these great works into practice. These works weren't just created so that their authors can make money; they are guides and blueprints left for us as a means to independence, sovereignty, and salvation. No melaninated face in the presidency is going to do that for us. Have you not learned from the lessons of Kwame Nkrumah, Patrice Lumumba, Maurice Bishop, or as recently as Jean Betrand Aristide? The man has to appease the political Powers-That-Be, and the Elite of this country; you don't think that they'll have him taken out if he even *thinks* about infringing on, or compromising on their imperialist interests? Don't be so gullible.

In the end, it is up to *us* to institute the change that is needed. We've been the answer that we've been searching for all along. The Honorable Marcus Garvey said it best: "Up you mighty race! You can accomplish what you will!"! It is the will of the people that will create the needed change in our collective lives. We must be unafraid in our commitment, and open-minded to these alternative theories and practices. It can be done...all we need to do is follow through on them.

MISCELLANEOUS ENTRIES

Hip Hopistas: Keep it Real!

By: Kevin Alberto Sabio

Although I have recently moved out of the state, I feel very fortunate to have been born and raised in New York City, the home of Hip Hop. I came of age in the '80s and early '90s, being able to receive the best of Hip Hop culture in its purest form. Having been born in the mid seventies, I was still too young to understand what was going on around me. I do remember the block parties, and the DJ's setting up their equipment in the local parks, tapping the street lights for a power source. I also remember seeing the pop lockers and the break dancers doing their thing at the jams. All I knew at the time was that this was really fun to watch, and that I had a *whole* lot of fun.

When the eighties came, and I was able to understand what was really happening, I relished in the fact that I was a witness to history in the making. It was about finding our own voice, and not having to follow the status quo. We didn't *have* to follow what was expected of us from mainstream (a/k/a WHITE) America; we could live and thrive on *our* terms. All of the brothers and sisters had embraced this music and culture with such a fervent passion that you almost *knew* that this was going to be something bigger than just a passing fad. I knew so many graf artists, breakers, lockers, emcees, and deejays that it would be an anomaly to *not* know anyone connected to the music and culture. Hip Hop influenced more than just a generation; its power is felt world wide!

Hip Hop is where I got my political start. The "Golden Era" of Hip Hop ('86-'93) had such influential emcees such as KRS-1, Rakim, Public Enemy, Bran Nubian, X Clan, Poor Righteous Teachers, and so many others that dropped political thought into their music. They talked about important Black figures in history that are almost *never* talked about, except in a negative way (Malcolm X, the Black Panthers, NOI, etc). My Latino classmates that I went to school with had a great respect for Black people, and Hip Hop music and culture (at least, MOST of them did). Having grown up together in pretty much the same neighborhoods, they also felt the sting of racism and prejudice, and recognized what time it was. The music also taught *them* to have pride in *their own* history and culture, and to not sell out to the mainstream society; you didn't have to assimilate, or die.

I also remember the Latino foray into the world of Rap music. There were some that were Afro-Latino and just basically 'passed'; being part of an ensemble rap group, and never playing up their nationality. I also remember the days of Mello Man Ace with his hit song "Mentirosa", and Kid Frost with his own jam "This is for La Raza". Def Jeff did his own thing in L.A., Latin Empire represented in New York, and it was all over by the time Cypress Hills hit the scene. Afterwards you had emcees like the Beatnuts, Fat Joe, Arsonists, Kurious Jorge, Lighter Shade of Brown, and many, many others since.

The pressing issue that *I* have started around the late 90's during that whole ridiculous 'Latin Explosion' phenomenon. I found it quite insulting, since Latino musicians have always been around.

I was a HUGE fan of Latin Freestyle during the eighties, not to mention listening to the music of Gloria Estefan and Jon Secada. What was really galling to me was the arrogance of certain newly arrived Latinos that had absolutely NO respect for Black people, and wanted to lay claim to Hip Hop music and Dance Hall. They wanted their due compensation, stating that if it wasn't for Latinos and their involvement, Hip Hop music and culture wouldn't exist. They also wanted to lay claim to the creation of Dance Hall Reggae music, saying that it wasn't a Jamaican-created music style, but a Puerto Rican creation. Basically…Black people didn't create ANYTHING… it was Latinos.

SAY *WHAT*?!?!?!?

I have actually seen a few articles in print stating this. Naturally, I grew *quite* upset when I had read them. First off…know your damn history. 1/3 of Latino culture is derived from AFRICANS! Second of all…Hip Hop music and culture is NOT youth culture… it's BLACK culture! Don't get it twisted! This isn't some corporate creation made by some office marketing team…WE created it! Just because mainstream America kissed your behind for a hot minute doesn't make you all of that. This is by no means an attack on all of my fellow Latinos; just the phonies who hopped on the bandwagon, and blatantly showed their prejudice and self hatred. That whole 'Latin Explosion' was nothing more than a whitewashing of who we are as a people. It's especially insidious for those newly arrived Latinos that show total disrespect to Black people without even knowing their history of struggle in this country! But yet, you want to blast *our* music, and rock *our* clothing styles, and speak using *our* street vernacular, right?

Gee…what gratitude….

For my true Hip Hopistas out there, you know who you are. You know the *true* history of the music and the culture. Don't let others who know nothing about the music (or the corporate vultures of the mainstream) denigrate and pimp our music and culture. Let all of the haters and perpetrators know what time it is. Don't let others profit off of what we've built, and twist the culture for their own personal agenda. It's not about gangsterism or miscegony, or violence and greed.

It's about self expression and knowledge of self…

It's about making your *own* way, not what society expects from you…

It's about having pride and self love…

It's about being true to yourself…

Just…keep it real!

The following was from a blog that I had written on my Myspace page, in response to a comment to Part II of the series "Black vs. Brown". The blog post was originally titled <u>Internet Assholes</u>...

For those of you who don't know, I am a contributing writer for an online magazine called Blacktino.net. They have given me the opportunity to express my view on certain subject matters as it pertains to racial issues. I have been writing a series of articles addressing the friction between the Black and Latino communities as of late called "Black vs. Brown". As an Afro Latino, the editors of the site felt that I could give a unique perspective on this particular issue.

On the Blacktino site, you are able to leave comments about the various articles that are posted. This is one particular comment that was left about one of my articles in the series:

Legitimate beef
2007-10-25 18:03:19

First of all I'd like to say that I can imagine how frustrating it is being a black Latino and not being recognized by lighter skinned Latinos. I am a black American born male who speaks Spanish fluently and sometimes and without an American accent and it is just amazing how I get so many stares when I speak at work or go out with one of my friends who is a mulatto Cuban.

The other part is that I live in Los Angeles and in my work in tourism I come in contact with many Latinos MOSTLY MEXICAN who will ofter come up to me and ask if I speak Spanish seemingly expecting me to say No so I can pass them off to someone lighter skin whom they'd feel more comfortable with. Or when I call the next person in line they hesitate and keep allowing people to cut in front of them so they can get to the lightest of our staff or the person whom they think "looks Latino." Alot of times these people end up being Ethiopian Egyptian or middle eastern since I work with a very diverse group of people. Nevertheless they are not to keen on being assisted by a dark skin person. Many people have tried to tell me that it has nothing to do with my color but it is a language barrier but I disagree. Many times these same Latinos "Mostly Mexican" once figuring out that light skin person is not Latino will began speaking English or continue speaking Spanglish as if they don't quite understand that when the person said "No Hablo Espanol" it was really the truth. When I speak to them in my fluent Spanish they freeze and often just stare at me or talk really slow assuming I don't understand.

I say all of this just to make a central point. Blacks have a very very legitimate beef about Latinos. I have traveled throughout much of central America including Honduras and have seen the sizable black populations in Costa Rica, Nicaragua Honduras and Guatemala. There a blacks over there who don't look mixed but are physically identical to their cousins of the African Diaspora, the black Americans. They are not the ones however leaving in droves as they do not have the economic resources and are financially deprived just as many black Americans here in the U.S.

That being said I do not support the illegal immigrants mostly Mexican because truth of the matter is if they were black Latinos entering the U.S. they would've been sent back a long time ago.

In addition, I find Latin America in general to be more racist and most have a tremendous color complex. By the way I live in Los Angeles where we have Mexicans who have never seen blacks before until coming to the U.S. You can't compare the black and latino experience in New York to the one in L.A. New York Hispanics are mainly from the Caribbean and include many Dominicans and Puerto Rican and although some of them might try to deny it, the fact is that many of them are black.

Here in L.A. we have Mexicans who are mostly "native Indian" racially. Think Aztec and Maya or indigenous to be politically correct. To them being black and the term "NEGRO" is some sort of taboo.

Needless to say they are scared of blacks and unlike the Puerto Rican and Dominican children of New York immigrants who mimmick African Americans through music, dance, and clothing the children of Mexican immigrants here in Los Angeles are forming gangs and shooting Africans Americans for no reason on our freeways. Like you said, we have a truly legitimate beef!

Frederick D. Young. (Registered)

Now...please excuse me as I commence to rip this asswipe a new one....

1) Nowhere in either of the two articles did I ever endorse illegal immigration. That's not the issue that I am talking about. A little reading comprehension would have told you that.

2) Mexicans aren't more racist than other Latinos. A racist Latino is a racist Latino REGRADLESS of their fucking nationality! Why do I always get some West Coast asswipe acting like they have the market cornered when it comes to racism from Latinos?!

3) That 'sizable' Black community that you're talking about in Latin America? They're called Garifuna. I should know...I **AM** a Garifuna! We are descended from the Maroons who escaped slavery. Oh...

they're not able to come to the US, unlike the other Latino ethnic groups? Come to New York asshole; all of the Garifuna are there! Honduran Garifuna, Belizian Garifuna...all of them. Please know what the fuck you are talking about before you fucking speak.

4) How the fuck you a Black man from the U.S. and have the fucking nerve to say that Latin America is <u>MORE RACIST</u> than the U.S.?!?!?!? What are you, fucking stupid?!!?!

5) For someone who has traveled all over Latin American, you don't know shit about it. You have Black people in Mexico. Every seen the Olmec heads? Ever visited Oaxaca, Guerrero, and Vera Cruz? Ever been to Costa Chica? You have indigenous Black communities out there.

The Indigenous community vastly outnumbers the African community in Latin America. If you had really traveled out there, you would know that. Even though you have a large African descended population in the Caribbean part of Latin America, that doesn't automatically mean that they're <u>ACCEPTING</u> of their African roots. You dumbass!!!!!

6) Yes, Black people do have a legitimate beef against Latinos. So do Latinos have a legitimate beef against Black people. The whole point of the article, if you read the shit properly, was that a lot of the friction between the two communities is mostly based on a) ignorance of each other, and b) the unfair distribution of resources by the power structure (White People) that keeps us fighting amongst ourselves and each other.

7) My old boss was Cuban. He was racist to the core. I know a lot of people who hate Cubans (specifically from Miami). You don't think that they shit on their fellow Afro Cubanos? I know many who will

back me up on that point. Your Cuban friend can kiss my liberated Black ass!

Please know what the fuck you are talking about before you fucking comment. I'm not interested in hearing/reading your racist rantings. Learn some fucking reading comprehension, and get your damn facts straight! Fucking dumbass!!!!

Please feel free to read all of my articles posted at Blacktino.net. The site is very informative, and up to date.

www.blacktino.net
www.community.blacktino.net

Notes: Since the time of the original posting of this post, the article series has been extended to 8 parts, and has been concluded with the eighth and final entry. The series goes as follows:

Black vs. Brown: Where's the Beef?
Black vs. Brown 2: The Next Level
Black vs. Brown 3: The Color Line
Black vs. Brown 4: Knowledge of Self
Black vs. Brown 5: History's Mystery
Black vs. Brown 6: Competition is None
Black vs. Brown 7: What's a Brother To Do?
Black vs. Brown 8: Internal Conflict (series end)

The following entry is from a blog posted on my MySpace page, regarding a confrontation that I got into online. The title of this particular blog is **Internet Assholes II**, and has been reposted on other profile pages as **ITGS (Internet Tough Guy/Girl Syndrome)**....

The following is an ongoing debate that I've been having on another networking site called <u>Black Authors Showcase</u>, *having a profile there to help promote the Black CapaCity Literary Arts Festival. The original forum discussion was about celebrating May as Latino Book Month. Due to the ignorance being spewed by the poster, I felt the need to respond....*

Reply by **Wizthom** on May 6, 2008 at 2:51pm

Latinos MM whom history only goes back 500,years, whats to celebrate other than the dislike they share for blacks, , there's a saying too many fires in the forest will start a blaze, i hear that latino compare their struggles to black struggles of civil rights, another false hood they stoled their way into this country they came of their own free will. just like the rest they wish to harvest civil right gains off the sweat and blood of my forfathers, sisters and brothers whom are still being held down „no thank u . peace wizthom i will pass

Reply by **Black CapaCity Literary Arts Festival** on May 8, 2008 at 5:34pm

Ummm....

Being a Latino, I take offense to your statement. Yes, some Latinos are prejudiced against Black people. That also means that they are prejudiced against themselves, considering that a good 1/3 of our culture derives from Africa. As a Latino of African descent (and

VERY proud of it), I've had to face prejudice and racism from "my own kind". They're just lost and ignorant.

Latinos aren't treated any better than Black people. You have this country's corrupt government exploiting the countries that Latinos come from, aside from the hell that they put the Black community through. If you really knew history, you would know that the two communities have actually worked together to fight oppression and racism. Ever heard of the Brown Berets and Young Lords Party? They were inspired by the Black Panther Party for Self Defense, and the groups have a documented history of working with each other. Also you had the work of the Hon. Marcus Garvey and the UNIA throughout Latin America.

Please, people....

Reply by **Wizthom**

i know ur history better than u do. the history that u are stating is not factual,,and i stand by what i wrote ,,to make a long story short,,visit any prison system or just watch lock up on tv and see for your self the workings as u say together of blacks and Latinos living in harmony, my friend,didn't mean to offend u,peace wizthom

Reply by **Black CapaCity Literary Arts Festival**

YOU don't know JACK!

What I'm stating isn't factual? There are plenty of documentaries and and books written by members of said groups that back me up. There are also other books written about the African heritage of Latinos. Want me to provide a list?

Prisons? That's the best comeback that you can throw at me...the prison system?! Give me friggin break! That's insulting my intelligence!

African weren't just brought to what eventual became the United States; this **ENTIRE HEMISPHERE** was a plantation system. Think I'm wrong? Do some research. A guy named Dr. Eric Williams would be a nice start. He wrote a number of books on the subject....

Don't talk out of your ass to me. You <u>don't</u> know me like that!

Reply by **Wizthom**

i gave u what ur level of intelligence could comprehend so i thought...

all races have the black gene in them, but that don't make them black .now don't insult my intelligence,as far as knowing you? you can't even control ur emotions,truth hurts only those who live a lie,i have nothing against you or your race .i just choose not to let you cut in line .peace wizthom ps watch Latino Latin Mexico,,now can go from there

Reply by **Wizthom**

i will not stoop to your level,when i enjoy having you look up to me, you are starting to bore me,,i still stand by this, Latinos MM whom history only goes back 500,years, whats to celebrate other than the dislike they share for blacks, , there's a saying too many fires in the forest will start a blaze, i hear that latino compare their struggles to black struggles of civil rights,

another false hood they stoled their way into this country they came of their own free will. just like the rest they wish to harvest civil right gains off the sweat and blood of my forfathers, sisters and brothers whom are still being held down „no thank u .

peace wizthom i will pass „if you are disliked by your own race then u must be too dark for them in that case we welcome you as we welcome the whites whom been rejected but it's wrong to compare yourself to American blacks just for political gain,peace wizthom

Reply by **Black CapaCity Literary Arts Festival**

if you are disliked by your own race then u must be too dark for them

1) Latino isn't a race, it's a culture. If you were so superior to me in intellect, you would have known that.

2) Did I say a 'black gene'? No. Africans were forcibly taken from the continent, and transported to the "New World". You know...the Middle Passage? The Maafa?

3) What level are you taking about...from the floor to my ass? I came at you with facts to back up my point. You have only come with conjecture and opinion. Not to mention that you're responses have been written atrociously.

4) There is racism within the Latino community. It's the result of our history with slavery. We have color complexes, and racial myths about "good hair/bad hair".

Go ahead, be bored. I've made my points. If you choose to be ignorant, then that's on you. I stand by the works of:

Dr. John H. Clarke
Dr. Arlene Torres
Dr. Victor Vega

Dr. Ivan Van Seritma

Runoko Rashisdi

Dr. Eric Williams

Juan Gonzalez

and many other ancestors and elders who came before me.

In Conclusion

My association with the E-zine Blacktino.net lasted from March 2007 through August 2008. During that time, I have had at least twenty of my articles posted on their site, including the two article series included in this book. Since my departure and disassociation from that site, I still continue with my political activism and writing career. I have ceased writing political commentary for the time being, and have gone back to my love of writing screenplays, and also having created a Literary Arts Festival representing for African descendents in the various fields and industry of literature. I am still an active member of the Universal Negro Improvement Association, though I am no longer associated with the Virginia division; I am in the process of relocating my efforts to Maryland, and joining our Maryland division. I still continue to fight for Black Nationalist/Pan Africanist causes as I always have, and still continue to include the voices and issues concerning my Afro Latino brethren.

I would like to give thanks to the many people that have supported me in all of my political and creative endeavors, for without your support, none of this would be possible. Of course, first and foremost, I thank the Creator for blessing me with the gift of expression through the written word. Without the blessing of this gift, none of my many works would exist before you.

DEFINITELY my parents Carlos and Raquel Sabio, my sister Ingrid, my brother Carlos, Boris, Enid, Tasha, niece Lashawn, and nephews Romello, Joshua, Miles, and Enrique....

To my dearest Michelle Gonzalez, who has always had my back from day one; you truly are the love of my life. I will love you always and forever....

To the many comrades and associates that I have been able to make through my activism; the UNIA-ACL, Jan Calloway, Delia "Afro Bori" Rodriguez, Dan Tres Omi, Chris Rodriguez, Miriam and Juan Flores and everyone from the Afrolatin@ Forum, The Los Afro Latinos Yahoo Group, Bruno Gaston, Karen Juanita Carrillo and Dr. Lisa Scott from Afropresencia.com, James "Moorbey" Harris from Black Unity, AssataShakur.org, Ezrah Aharone, Khadijah Ali-Coleman from Liberated Muse, Diane Williams from Black Author Showcase, Kellie Williams from SoJournals.com, Terra Renee from African American Women in Cinema film festival, The Defenders for Freedom Justice and Equality, Robert Oriyama'at (my Bridgeport homie!!!), Afi Makalani (keep spitting them hot lyrics!!!!), Sis. Amachi Truth & Koblah Atiba, Etaniel Yehuda, President General Senghor Jawara Baye, Bro. Babatunji Balogun, Julie Williamson, Felicia Pride, Savannah J, Ron "R Jay Jay" Johnson, Steven Van Patten, Jemir Johnson, Angel Mechelle Mitchell and her brother Fred Mitchell, Barbara Holguin, Alicia Anabel Santos and her peoples at Creador Pictures (the documentary looks HOT!!!), Crystal S. Roman from Black Latina Movement LLC, Dr. Marta Moreno-Vega and the crew of the Caribbean Cultural Center and African Diaspora Institute, Stan "Substantial" Robinson (one of THE sickest emcees on the planet), Be One (one of THE illest femcees on the planet), Lynx Garcia, Sofia Quintero, my dear friend Linda Haynes, and all my RBG souljahs, sistas, y todo mis guerreristas revolutionistas.....

This is only the beginning......

CPSIA information can be obtained at www.ICGtesting.com
Printed in the USA
BVOW03s0057300514

354859BV00001B/28/P